Great Garden Gadgets

Great Garden Gadgets

Make-It-Yourself Gizmos and Projects

Fern Marshall Bradley and Christine Bucks, Editors

RODALE

RODALE

WE INSPIRE AND ENABLE PEOPLE TO IMPROVE
THEIR LIVES AND THE WORLD AROUND THEM

LIBRARY OF CONGRESS CATALOGING-IN-PUBLICATION DATA

    Great garden gadgets : make-it-yourself gizmos and projects / Fern Marshall Bradley and Christine Bucks, editors.

         p.   cm.

    Includes bibliographical references (p.) and index.

    ISBN 0–87596–998–4   (pbk. : alk. paper)

    1. Garden tools—Design and construction—Amateurs' manuals.   2. Garden ornaments and furniture—Design and construction—Amateurs' manuals. I. Bradley, Fern Marshall. II. Title.

SB454.8 .G74 2001

635.9'1—dc21   2001000794

Distributed in the book trade by St. Martin's Press

2 4 6 8 10 9 7 5 3 1   paperback

Editors: Fern Marshall Bradley and Christine Bucks
Contributing Editors: Karen Bolesta, Tony O'Malley, Nancy Ondra, Karen Costello Soltys
Cover and Interior Designer: Marta Mitchell Strait
Contributing Designer: Dale Mack
Cover and Interior Illustrators: John and Linda Gist
Layout Designer: Jennifer H. Giandomenico
Researchers: Claudia Curran, Diana Erney, Sarah Wolfgang Heffner
Copy Editors: Stacey Ann Follin, Candace Levy
Manufacturing Coordinator: Patrick T. Smith
Indexer: Lina Burton
Editorial Assistance: Kerrie A. Cadden

RODALE ORGANIC GARDENING BOOKS

Executive Editor: Kathleen DeVanna Fish
Managing Editor: Fern Marshall Bradley
Executive Creative Director: Christin Gangi
Art Director: Patricia Field
Production Manager: Robert V. Anderson Jr.
Studio Manager: Leslie M. Keefe
Copy Manager: Nancy N. Bailey
Book Manufacturing Director: Helen Clogston

We're always happy to hear from you. For questions or comments concerning the editorial content of this book, please write to:

    Rodale Book Readers' Service
    33 East Minor Street
    Emmaus, PA 18098

Look for other Rodale books wherever books are sold. Or call us at (800) 848-4735.

For more information about Rodale Organic Gardening magazine and books, visit us at

www.organicgardening.com

Rodale

ORGANIC GARDENING STARTS HERE!

Here at Rodale, we've been gardening organically for more than 50 years—ever since my grandfather J. I. Rodale learned about composting and decided that healthy living starts with healthy soil. In 1940 J. I. started the Rodale Organic Farm to test his theories, and today the nonprofit Rodale Institute Experimental Farm is still at the forefront of organic gardening and farming research. In 1942 J. I. founded *Organic Gardening* magazine to share his discoveries with gardeners everywhere. His son, my father, Robert Rodale, headed *Organic Gardening* until 1990, and today a fourth generation of Rodales is growing up with the magazine. Over the years we've shown millions of readers how to grow bountiful crops and beautiful flowers using nature's own techniques.

In this book, you'll find the latest organic methods and the best gardening advice. We know—because all our authors and editors are passionate about gardening! We feel strongly that our gardens should be safe for our children, pets, and the birds and butterflies that add beauty and delight to our lives and landscapes. Our gardens should provide us with fresh, flavorful vegetables, delightful herbs, and gorgeous flowers. And they should be a pleasure to work in as well as to view.

Sharing the secrets of safe, successful gardening is why we publish books. So come visit us at the Rodale Institute Experimental Farm, where you can tour the gardens every day—we're open year-round. And use this book to create your best garden ever.

Happy gardening!

Maria Rodale

Maria Rodale
Rodale Organic Gardening Books

Contents

Contributors

Rob Cardillo, a former editor for *Organic Gardening* magazine, is currently a freelance writer and photographer for a number of publications. His front yard features flowering alliums, unusual shrubs, and a sprinkling of edible greens.

George DeVault is the editor of Rodale's Russian-language gardening and farming magazine. He operates a certified organic vegetable farm in Emmaus, Pennsylvania.

Nancy Engel tends a half-acre garden in Putnam County, New York, where she faces the daily challenges of deer, rocks, and roving cats and dogs.

Mike Ferrara is a product consultant and spokesperson for major companies in the home improvement market. He currently appears on HGTV and other networks as "The Lazy Homeowner," informing viewers about the latest timesaving tools available.

Veronica Lorson Fowler is an Ames, Iowa-based freelance garden writer and editor. She has contributed to various national publications, including *Better Homes and Gardens*, and is also a Master Gardener.

Linda Harris is a horticultural writer, desktop designer of Web sites and catalogs, marketing consultant, Master Gardener, and speaker. She's currently working on a book about birds and butterflies.

Sally McCabe is an outreach coordinator for the Pennsylvania Horticultural Society's Philadelphia Green. She's also on the board of the American Community Gardening Association. Sally has worked in community gardening for more than 25 years and has recycled 5-gallon buckets for most of that time.

Pat Michalak has an M.S. in entomology and a B.S. in crop and soil science from Michigan State University. She's currently an entomologist who works with wholesale greenhouse growers to reduce their pest problems.

Barbara Pleasant lives and gardens in Huntsville, Alabama. She is the author of a dozen gardening books and more magazine articles and newspaper columns than she can remember.

Melinda Rizzo is a freelance writer living and gardening in Upper Bucks County, Pennsylvania.

Sally Roth is the author of *The Backyard Bird Feeder's Bible, Attracting Butterflies and Hummingbirds to Your Backyard,* and several other books.

Warren Schultz is the author of 12 books, including *The Organic Suburbanite* and *A Man's Garden*. Formerly editor-in-chief of *National Gardening* and features editor of *Garden Design*, he now lives and gardens in South Burlington, Vermont.

Vicki Webster is the author of numerous books and magazine articles and has also written extensively for electronic media. She's a former editor at *Country Home* and *Better Homes and Gardens* magazines and is currently a book editor at Storey Books.

A Gadget a Day

A great garden gadget is an exciting find. You spot them occasionally in garden catalogs or at your local garden center, but the best gadgets are the nifty homemade widgets that your friends have devised. You know what we mean—a planter made from a milk jug and a piece of plastic pipe, a plastic soda bottle modified to be a watering reservoir, pieces of plastic miniblinds recycled as plant markers.

Gardeners get revved up about gadgets because they can help save time, make tricky jobs simpler, give new life to cast-off items, and just make gardening more fun!

We love homemade garden contrivances, too, and that's why we decided to create a book filled with terrific gadget ideas. Our writers tracked down nifty gizmos, recycled doodads, and inventive garden accessories from every part of the country and for nearly every garden task—from making compost and planting seeds to controlling weeds and trellising climbing plants.

This is a great book for browsing, and we hope you'll enjoy sampling a homemade tool idea here and an ingenious frost protection apparatus there. If you're looking for ideas to help you with a particular task, check the table of contents. You'll find we've grouped similar gadgets together in chapters such as Storage Savers and Tool Organizers, Lawn and Landscape Tools, Feeding and Watering Helpers, and more.

START OUT SIMPLE

If the idea of making your own gadgets seems a little intimidating, start by searching for the "Recycle It!" logo. That's your clue to fast-and-easy devices and garden helpers you can make using materials that you probably have on hand in your house, garage, or garden shed.

For example, one gardener uses a scrap piece of wire mesh fencing as a "stepping-stone" near the water spigot to provide firm footing without puddling. Another has turned an old fisherman's vest into a gardener's vest complete with marking pens, plant labels, and seeds. You're sure to find plenty of great new uses for those gardener's standards: milk jugs, soda bottles, scraps of wood, and old panty hose!

LOOKING FOR A CHALLENGE?

Gardeners with a bent for building should watch for the "Build It!" logo throughout these pages. Every "Build It!" offers step-by-step instructions for each detail in constructing more elaborate creations like a tool caddy fashioned from boards and dowels or a trellis made from twigs and baling twine.

When it comes to more complex gadgets, we know that a picture truly *is* worth a thousand words, so we've included a generous dose of illustrations to show how to make and use many of the more intricate structures and implements in the book.

You'll store up a treasure trove of great ideas for your garden as you read *Great Garden Gadgets*. Perhaps you'll be inspired with some great ideas of your own! If you do, we'd love to know about them, and you can tell us about them through the Gardener to Gardener forum at www.organicgardening.com. Sign on, and we'll have a gadgets chat!

Bird-Feeding Gadgets

Want to attract more birds to your yard? Try to create prime habitat in your backyard by making a plastic netting suet bag, gourd birdhouse, or an instant birdbath. Tired of starlings taking over your purple martin house? Duct tape may be the answer to your problem. Read on to learn how a few simple gadgets can help bring the right birds to your yard.

NET BAGS FOR SUET AND SUPPLIES

Use plastic netting bags from onions or citrus fruit to offer suet to birds in winter, suggests Linda Harris of Fulton, Kentucky. Here's how she does it: Place suet in the bag and tie a knot at the top. Cut the hook section off a wire clothes hanger, and bend it open into a single straight length of wire. Run the wire through the bag just under the knot. Bend the wire into a U-shape, twist the ends together, and then hang the bag on a tree branch near your house windows so you can watch birds feed.

In early spring, fill another bag with pet hair, longish human hair, 6-inch lengths of string, straw, or small clippings of plant material from your garden, and hang it up in the same way. Birds will help themselves to these nest-building materials and will thank you by nesting nearby.

DUCT TAPE SAYS "NO VACANCY"

Purple martins are wonderful residents of any backyard, both for their beauty and song as well as for their assistance in insect control. But these flying bug catchers face stiff competition from house sparrows, which often usurp their apartment houses before the martins return from migration.

Birdhouse suppliers market various guards to close off apartment entrances, but martin fancier Connie Wilson of Mt. Vernon, Indiana, found a simpler solution to keep out the unwanteds. "I just stick a piece of duct tape over the holes until I see the first martin scout arrive. Then I remove the tape so the martins can move in."

INSTANT BIRDBATH

Every garden should have a birdbath, but store-bought birdbaths can cost a pretty penny. Rather than buying a birdbath, Janet

ON HAND: Old cracked concrete birdbath without its base

TURN IT INTO: Ground-level bird feeder and sanctuary

HOW TO DO IT: Dig a slight depression in a flowerbed and set in the birdbath saucer. Place a little bowl of water or fruit in the middle and pour seed around it.

ON HAND: Old door mat

TURN IT INTO: Birdseed catcher

HOW TO DO IT: Put a scrap of door mat under the bird feeder and on top of fresh snow so seed falls on it and not into the snow where the birds can't get to them.

Carter, outreach coordinator at the Pennsylvania Horticultural Society's Philadelphia Green, recommends that gardeners take a round drainage tray for a potted plant (10 to 12 inches in diameter is best) and place it onto the top of a sturdy tomato cage (a four-legged cage is stronger than a three-legged one). The birdbath will hold about 2 inches of water without wobbling and you can easily move it around the garden, so you can find the places the birds like best. Smaller, shorter, and shallower models work great in butterfly and rock gardens.

A DRAINAGE TRAY FILLED WITH 2 INCHES OF WATER AND PLACED ON TOP OF A TAPERED THREE- OR FOUR-LEGGED TOMATO CAGE WILL PROVIDE THE BIRDS THAT FREQUENT YOUR GARDEN WITH A SOURCE OF WATER.

Build It!

GOURD BIRDHOUSE

If you like interesting and appealing birdhouses to adorn your garden and welcome your feathered friends, here's a way to grow and make your own. Grow large bottle-type gourds (sometimes called birdhouse gourds) and harvest them when they're fully mature (or just before frost hits, whichever comes first). Plan to grow them on a trellis, which helps keep the fruits rounded and at their best. When you harvest, leave several inches of stem on each fruit.

"I've seen these gourd birdhouses painted white and hung in colonies for martins," says Linda Harris of Fulton, Kentucky, "but I think it's best to leave the gourds untreated and unpainted, to avoid any possible toxic effect on the birds who'll be nesting in the gourd."

Materials

1 dried large gourd

¼-inch-diameter wooden dowel, 3 inches long

Permanent glue

12 to 18 inches of sturdy twine or cord

Narrow-bladed saw or sharp X-Acto knife

Electric drill with ¼-inch bit

DIRECTIONS

1. Harvest the gourd and hang it to dry, or place it on chicken wire or hardware cloth in a warm, airy, sheltered spot. When a gourd has thoroughly dried (which may take several months), it will be tan, and you can shake it and hear the dried flesh and seeds rattle.

2. Using a pencil, draw a 1-inch-diameter circle for the door about one-third of the way up from the bottom of the gourd. Carefully saw or cut through the gourd shell, following the pencil line, then remove the circle of shell. Shake out the flesh and seeds. Save the seeds to grow more gourds.

3. Drill a ¼-inch-diameter hole about 1 inch below the door. Insert the dowel in the hole so about 1 inch is inside the gourd. Apply glue to the circle where the dowel and gourd meet, and then let the glue dry thoroughly.

4. Drill a ¼-inch hole on both sides of the gourd about 2 inches from the top of the gourd. Insert twine through both holes, and tie the ends together in a knot.

5. Hang your birdhouse in a tree before spring nesting begins, and watch for visitors.

1" DIAMETER CIRCLE

WOODEN DOWEL

On hand: Ceramic cup with a broken handle

Turn it into: A miniature bird and butterfly bath

How to do it: Sink the cup to its rim in the soil of a flowerbed or border, and fill the cup with water.

H₂O for Beneficials

The beneficial insects in your garden need water just as much as birds, but birdbaths don't serve the needs of ants, spiders, and beetles. Jeff Ball, a garden writer from West Chester, Pennsylvania, came up with a way to keep insects hydrated, too. He created a bug watering can.

"The bug watering can is nothing more than an empty tuna fish or cat food can stuffed with a plastic pot scrubber (netting bunched up into a ball)," says Ball. "The plastic scrubber lets the insects get down to the water without worrying about falling in. I have at least six of these bug watering cans situated in out-of-the-way places around my garden. The rain will usually keep them filled, but when the drought comes, the bug cans get filled with water right along with the birdbath."

Cat Litter Is for the Birds

Heavy bags of birdseed are economical to buy, but hard to handle. And, once they're opened, mice or squirrels can make a feast on birdseed you store in a shed or garage. Today, some cat litter brands are available in handy plastic buckets with lids. So if you have a cat or two, switch to the economy-size bucket of litter. Once the litter pail is empty, rinse it out, dry it thoroughly, and use it as a secure storage bucket for birdseed. Says Karen Soltys of Sellersville, Pennsylvania, "Toss in a scoop, and you can carry the bucket of seed to any of your feeders and scoop out what you need. It's much easier than lugging a 20-pound bag of sunflower seed and hoisting it up to the feeder. The snap-on lid helps keep the seed fresh, too."

Compost-Making Equipment

Every great garden starts with good soil. One of the ways to create good soil is by amending your beds with lots of compost. But there's no reason to shed sweat and tears while producing that black gold. Read on to find out what gadgets your fellow gardeners use to make composting a snap.

SOLVE THE RIDDLE PROBLEM

Compost sieves, sometimes called riddles, tend to be small and expensive, but you can easily build one of your own that fits on top of your wheelbarrow—for just a few dollars. This sieve and wheelbarrow setup is perfect for resting next to the compost pile where you can scoop compost on top and work it through the screen with a trowel or spade. The resulting fine-textured compost is ideal for adding to indoor plants, starting seedlings, and doing other container gardening.

To make the sieve, nail four pieces of lumber, such as 1 × 2s, into a large square or rectangle big enough to rest across the wheelbarrow with a few inches to spare. Then use snips to cut a piece of galvanized hardware cloth to fit the wood frame. Attach the hardware cloth to the bottom of the frame with galvanized brads.

MAKE YOUR OWN FINE-TEXTURED COMPOST WITH AN INEXPENSIVE, BUILD-IT-YOURSELF SIEVE.

EASY COMPOST AERATOR

Tired of spending hours turning your compost pile to keep it well aerated? Kelly Winterton of Mountain Green, Utah, discovered the perfect

ON HAND: Net onion bag

TURN IT INTO: Compost tea bag

HOW TO DO IT: When opening your next bag of onions, untie the string gathered at the top rather than ripping through the netting. Fill the bag with compost, retie it, and place it in a bucket of water. Allow it to steep for a week or more, then use the liquid to water plants and give them a fertilizer boost.

the compost. Les made the compost sieve out of ½-inch rabbit mesh and four 2 × 2s. "I placed the sieve across the top of my wheelbarrow and shoveled on the compost," says Martha, "but getting the compost to go through the screen was quite a job. So Les found an old handheld vibrating sander and used some wire to attach the sander to the rabbit mesh. We turned on the sander, started shoveling, and the compost went through quickly and easily." (*Note:* For safety's sake, make sure you plug the sander into a grounded GFCI outlet.)

A HANDHELD VIBRATING SANDER ADDS JUST ENOUGH SHAKE, RATTLE, AND ROLL TO GET COMPOST THROUGH A SIEVE EASILY.

compost tool right in his garden shed: a bulb-planting auger designed to be used with a cordless drill. Winterton just hooks up the auger, turns on the drill, and pushes the business end through the compost pile. The auger easily makes channels for air to enter the pile. As a bonus, the auger mixes and chops the materials as it works, speeding up the composting process.

SHIMMYING COMPOST SIEVE

Martha Black and her husband, Les, of Anchorage, Alaska, came up with a vibrating compost sieve to make quick work of screening

COMPOSTING TOMATO CAGES

Tomatoes and peppers love rich soil. Help them thrive by providing them with their own supply of compost! Make a cylinder from a 6-foot length of wire fencing (chicken wire or varying grades of turkey wire are fine; just be

Build It!

BUS TUB WORM BIN

A worm bin is a great way to make rich, odorless compost indoors. You can spend $100 or more to buy a commercial worm bin kit, or you can do what Kelly Houston of San Francisco, California, did and make your own bin. Houston started with two "bus tubs" (containers used to gather up dirty dishes) from the restaurant where she works. Chances are you can buy them from a local restaurant supply company, or you can buy similar-size utility bins from a discount store.

Materials

2 plastic tubs (each about 18 × 14 × 12 inches deep)

Chicken wire

1 tub lid

Black paint

About 1,000 red worms

Kitchen scraps (no citrus, potato peels, fat, bones, or eggshells)

Damp, shredded newspaper

Sturdy box or milk crate

Large jar or 2-liter soda bottle with top cut off

Electric drill with ¼-inch bit

Utility knife

Staple gun

DIRECTIONS

1. Drill ¼-inch-diameter ventilation holes in a line parallel to and 4 inches below the top of each tub.

2. Cut the bottom from one of the tubs with the utility knife, and staple chicken wire over the bottom. This will be the worm tub.

3. Paint the tub lid black to keep light out.

4. Place red worms and kitchen scraps in worm tub, and cover completely with damp, shredded newspaper.

5. With the utility knife, cut a 1-inch-wide drain hole at a low point on one side of the bottom of the other tub. This will be the drain tub.

6. Cover the worm tub with the black lid, and place it inside the drain tub.

7. Set the assembled setup on top of a sturdy box or old milk crate, and place the large jar or 2-liter soda bottle under the drain hole.

"When there's a noticeable amount of worm castings in the worm tub, I lift it out and dump everything into the drain tub," Houston says. "Then I place the empty tub back into the bottom tub, right on top of the compost, and start over with new scraps in the empty tub, covering them well with damp newspaper strips. I empty the jar once in a while and water my houseplants with it." The worms will gradually move up through the wire mesh to where the "fresh" food scraps are; then you can harvest the compost in the lower tub without losing too many worms. After harvesting the lower tub, she places the worm tub back in the empty drain tub and begins again.

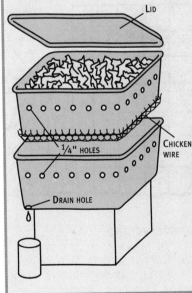

LID

¼" HOLES

CHICKEN WIRE

DRAIN HOLE

ON HAND: 5-gallon or larger bucket with lid

TURN IT INTO: Direct composter

HOW TO DO IT: Cut out the bucket's bottom with a pair of heavy-duty shears or a utility knife. Push the bucket into one of your garden beds so the bottom of the bucket is 12 inches below the soil surface. Add compost, weeds without seeds, and plant wastes every day (no meat or processed food, please!). Keep the lid on to avoid attracting flies and other critters. When it's nearly full, pull the bucket up and cover the pile with soil. It will quickly settle as the compost rots and the earthworms do their work—and, as the compost breaks down, it will provide the bed with nutrients. Tomatoes and squash-family crops, both heavy feeders, will benefit greatly when planted close by.

sure it can stand without support). You can cut 5-foot-wide fencing in half to make a pair of 2½-foot-high cages—this height is visually unobtrusive but is still high enough to stake tomatoes. Cut the vertical wires in an alternating pattern to provide tinelike feet that will stick into the dirt. Clamp the cages closed with small pieces of wire coat hanger or extra pieces of fencing. Place the cage in a garden bed and use it to hold garden wastes, especially weeds.

As plant scraps break down, they'll directly feed plants growing near them, so plant tomatoes, peppers, or vine crops around the outside of the cylinder, and train them to grow up the sides of the fencing. At the end of the season, pull up the wire cylinder, shake off the dead vines, and move it to another section of the garden. Begin filling it again as you do your fall cleanup.

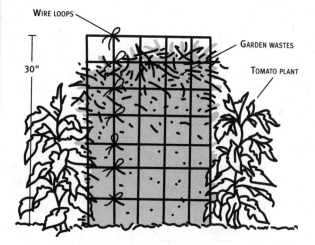

USE WIRE FENCING AND COAT-HANGER WIRE LOOPS TO MAKE A COMPOSTING CAGE FOR YOUR TOMATOES AND PEPPERS. THEY'LL THRIVE ON THE RICH SOIL THAT THE COMPOST PROVIDES.

Build It!

LATTICE COMPOST BIN

Wooden lattice is a nice choice for screening around the base of a deck, and if you have some leftover sheets of lattice from a deck renovation project, use them around your compost. You can build a handsome two-bin compost structure from three sheets of lattice and a few scrap 2 × 4s. And it will only take about 3 hours from start to finish.

Materials

Three 4 × 8-foot sheets of lattice

Six 5-foot 2 × 4s

6-penny galvanized nails or 1-inch galvanized screws

Four 4-foot wooden slats

Level

Hammer or screwdriver

DIRECTIONS

1. Cut two 4 × 8-foot sheets of lattice in half to make four panels, each 4 × 4 foot. (Only three panels are needed.)

2. Sink four 2 × 4s 1 foot deep in the ground to form the corners of a 4 × 8-foot rectangle. Use a level to set them straight.

3. Sink one 2 × 4 at the midpoint of each of the long sides of the rectangle.

4. Nail or screw the remaining 4 × 8-foot lattice panel to the 2 × 4s on one long side to form the back wall of the bin.

5. Make side walls by nailing one 4 × 4-foot panel between the 2 × 4s on each end.

6. Create a slot on the inside of each center 2 × 4 by nailing two slats parallel to each other onto the 2 × 4. Allow enough room in between for lattice to fit between them. (See detail.)

7. Slide a 4 × 4-foot panel into the slots to create a center wall.

8. When it's time to turn or move the compost, simply slide the center lattice out and go at it!

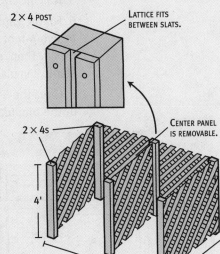

CENTER POST DETAIL

2 × 4 POST

LATTICE FITS BETWEEN SLATS.

2 × 4s

CENTER PANEL IS REMOVABLE.

4'

8'

4'

Build It!

A Simple Double Compost Bin

Ed Preneta of Unionville, Connecticut, put together a simple two-bin compost "corral" that has held up for almost 15 years. Though it's decidedly low-tech, it has proven secure enough to keep out deer, fox, coyotes, and even black bear. A removable front gate allows him to stack the bins full of compost material, yet it gives him access when it's time to turn or harvest the compost.

Materials

Twenty-six 4-foot 2 × 4s

6-penny galvanized nails

Dog wire

Two 8-foot 2 × 4s

Chicken wire

Two 5-foot-tall metal stakes

Bird netting

Hammer

Staple gun

Directions

1. Nail twelve 4-foot 2 × 4s together to form a simple 4 × 4 × 4-foot frame (as shown).

2. Repeat to construct a second frame.

3. Wrap dog wire around three sides of each frame, and staple in place.

4. On a level surface, place the frames next to each other so the open ends are side by side, forming one 8-foot, open-sided double bin.

5. Nail the two frames together.

6. For the gate, nail the two 8-foot 2 × 4s to two 4-foot 2 × 4s to form a 4 × 8-foot frame. Then, cover it with chicken wire, and staple it in place.

7. Drive the 5-foot stakes into the ground at the front corners of the bin, leaving about 2 inches of clearance between the stakes and the bin.

8. Slide the gate between a stake and the corner of the bin, until both ends are held in place by the stakes.

The stakes hold the gate firmly in place, but when it's time to turn the compost, Preneta simply slides the gate away from the front of the bin. He also drapes bird netting over top of the bin to keep the birds from robbing his precious compost.

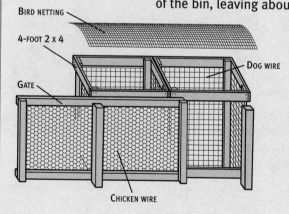

BIRD NETTING

4-FOOT 2 x 4

GATE

DOG WIRE

CHICKEN WIRE

Homemade Hand Tools

Hoes, shovels, trowels, rakes. So many tools to choose from — so little time. Even though gardening tools don't last forever, you can revamp and refurbish your tools to make them last twice as long. The following tips will help you keep your favorite tools (and your hands) usable in the years to come.

A BETTER AX

Tired of swinging a heavy, clumsy mattock to remove sod, chop roots and stumps, or break up hard soil? "Try a Pulaski," advises 74-year-old Don DeVault of Delaware, Ohio. "It's a lightweight ax that firefighters use in forest fires and brush fires. It's about half the weight of a normal mattock." The Pulaski has an ax blade on one side and a scaled-down mattock on the other. "It's great for edging, lifting sod, and chopping roots. My firefighter son gave me one for Christmas," DeVault says. "I can use it all day in the garden and woods." (See "Resources" on page 144 for ordering information.)

SHEAR GLADNESS

Like many great inventions, Frederick Theilig's favorite garden gadget came from a misguided attempt to solve a problem. The problem? A large Christmas tree that had to be removed from a small room in their Cranston, Rhode Island, apartment. Rather than dragging the tree intact through the door and scattering pine needles everywhere, Theilig decided that the best way to get it out of the apartment after the holiday would be to cut the branches from the trunk. So, he grabbed the nearest cutting tool—a pair of scissors. Too bad they were his wife Sona's best kitchen shears.

It worked. In no time at all, those sturdy 8-inch-long shears had reduced the tree to a trunk and a pile of boughs. As proud as he was of his creative thinking, he found that Sona wasn't pleased, so Fred bought her a belated Christmas present: a new pair of shears. That meant that he could take full possession of the old ones.

Several years later, the shears remain among his favorite tools. "I still use them to harvest tomatoes, peas, beans, and similar small-stemmed fruit," he says "They're strong, conveniently sized, and relatively cheap, and you can find them at any kitchen store. They even have a notch for cutting bones, which is perfect for pruning the smaller growth on shrubs and trees. I also use them for deadheading and killing tough weedy vines and have even used them to trim plastic mulch."

Nothing seems to dull or harm the stainless-steel shears. "They've survived three intense seasons in the garden without significantly dulling," Fred says.

THE CUTTING EDGE

Tired of trying to pry apart tough perennial clumps when dividing them? Gayle Jamison of Woodstock, New York, keeps a long-bladed, stainless steel, serrated kitchen knife handy for dividing perennials. "It works great for all sorts of divisions," she says, "such as for grasses, daylilies, hostas, and even more delicate root structures that don't pull apart easily." She sometimes even leaves the plant in the ground and just saws off a section of it, to minimize trauma to the parent plant.

A serrated bread knife also can be extremely useful and versatile in the garden. It's great for separating plants in a flat, and particularly for cutting heavy plastic pots to release potbound plants. You can also use it to trim the roots of potted plants and to divide water lilies.

ON HAND: Net bags, such as those that onions, potatoes, and citrus come in

TURN THEM INTO: "Pot scrubbers" for cleaning tools

HOW TO DO IT: "Just cut off a chunk of the bag," says Lon Rombough of Aurora, Oregon, "or for larger tools, such as a shovel, use the whole bag." Rombough wads up the mesh bag and goes to town. "When you're finished cleaning, just unwad and shake out the bag."

NEW LIFE FOR OLD TOOLS

When the handle of a favorite long-handled tool breaks, don't throw the tool out. "Turn it into a short-handled tool that you might like even better," say Sandy and Dennis "Bones" Evers of Bayfield, Colorado.

If the handle broke in the middle, the tool transformation is super simple. Just saw it off and sand the rough edges. A tool that breaks at the business end is a little more difficult to modify, but it can be done.

1. Remove the wood from the metal part of the tool. You can either drill it out with a power drill or toss it in a fire, Bones says. (If you toss it in a fire and burn the remnant out, the metal may lose some of its temper but may still be good for years.)
2. Cut the remaining handle to the desired length. Taper it so it will fit into the metal part either by whittling it with a knife or sanding it.
3. Attach the two parts by standing the handle on a hard surface and placing the metal portion atop that. Holding onto the tool

end, give it a good rap against the floor several times to force the parts together.

4. If there's a hole in the tool's shank, work a screw or nail into it to further secure the new handle.

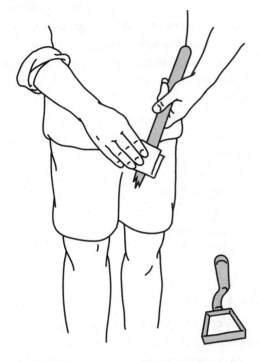

IF A TOOL HANDLE BREAKS, REMOVE THE WOODEN STUB FROM THE METAL PART OF THE TOOL. SAND DOWN THE HANDLE AND FIT IT BACK INTO THE TOOL HEAD.

TWO TOOLS FROM ONE

How many of us have snapped a hoe handle in half, either through overaggressive hoeing or in a fit of pique at an exceptionally recalcitrant weed? When that happens, we normally toss it in the trash and head to the hardware store to buy a new hoe. But Jo Meller and Jim Sluyter of Five Springs Farm in Bear Lake, Michigan, don't like to waste anything, so they decided to make the most of their broken tool. In fact, they turned one broken tool into two usable ones.

First, Jo and Jim took the bladed end of the hoe, which had about 18 inches of the handle left, and cut off the broken edges of the handle with a saw. Then they filed the end smooth, which left them with a short-handled hoe. To make it even easier to use the hoe in tight spots, Sluyter filed the blade down with a grinder so that it's 3 inches wide.

Then they turned their attention to the remaining piece of the broken handle. Again, using a saw, Jim cut the handle down to a 12-inch length. Using a rasp, he filed the end to a point and, voilà, "a pretty good dibble, big enough for large bulbs and suitable for the large plantings of garlic that we make every year," Sluyter says. "I made a better dibble, some years later, when the D-grip handle of a shovel broke—the D-grip handle makes it much more pleasant to work with."

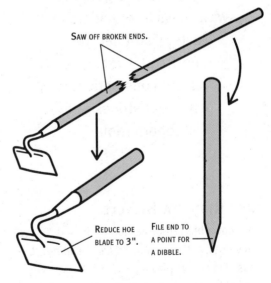

SAW OFF BROKEN ENDS.

REDUCE HOE BLADE TO 3".

FILE END TO A POINT FOR A DIBBLE.

FIND NEW LIFE FOR A BROKEN HOE BY TURNING THE PIECES INTO A SHORT-HANDLED HOE AND A DIBBLE.

On hand: An old hoe

Turn it into: A useful hand tool

How to do it: Cut the end off so the remaining handle is about 18 inches long, and sand the end smooth. "This shorter tool is great for close-up jobs when you want good leverage and a broad surface without a long handle to get in the way," says Jerry Anderson, Master Gardener from Portland, Oregon. "I use it constantly for prying out stones and stubborn roots."

Like Riding a Bicycle

"I'm not a big fan of gardening gloves," says Sally Roth, author of *Natural Landscaping*, "because I'm always playing with plants even while I'm raking or digging, and gloves make me fumble-fingered. But I'm prone to blisters when I do intensive garden work with a rake or hoe, so I was forever putting gloves on and taking them off."

After moving her son's bike out of the way so she could rake the fall leaves, inspiration struck. "Those fat, cushy, foam handlebar grips were so nice to hold after an hour of work with a wood-handled rake. I knew my son added the grips to the handlebar himself—and the handlebar was almost the same size as my tool handle."

Roth made a quick trip to a nearby store for the inexpensive handlebar grips, and wiggled the hollow foam tubes onto the handles of her rake and hoe, where they fit snugly. "Now my tools are so comfortable, I never worry about blisters, no matter how long I work," she says. "I even added a handlebar grip to my household broom."

"Pinch" Perennials in a Hurry

Many perennials—including fall asters, mums, garden phlox, agastache, and others—push out vigorous side branches when the tip of the growing stem is nipped off, and that means more flowers from each plant plus a denser form. But nipping off the tips of dozens or hundreds of stems can be a tedious task.

"Pinching the tips of perennials gives me at least double the amount of flowers," says gardener Sally Roth of New Harmony, Indiana, "but my gardens get bigger every year, and it's harder to keep up when I pinch each stem by hand. I switched to hedge clippers a few years ago, and they're perfect. I can clip off the tips of an entire clump of phlox with just one or two swipes of the clippers."

Try this technique when your perennials are 6 to 12 inches tall, with at least four sets of leaves on the stem. You'll find it's easy to slice through the stems while they're still green.

ELECTRICAL TAPE RECHARGES AN OLD TOOL

"I abuse my shovels regularly," says Sally Roth, who has been gardening since she was 2 years old. "They aren't made to be crowbars, I know, but I just can't restrain myself from using them to lever out heavy shrubs or trees. Even the most expensive ones crack a handle now and then."

When she hears that telltale sound of splitting wood, Roth reaches for a roll of black electrical tape and performs emergency surgery on the spot. "The tape fits nice and snug to the handle and isn't irritating to my hand when I'm using the tool," she says, noting that patched shovels get retired to the light-duty section of the tool shed. "They still have years of good use in them. I save them for easier jobs, like moving perennials or loosening the vegetable garden soil." If you don't have electrical tape on hand, turn to that old standby, duct tape. It's wider, stickier, and less slippery than electrical tape.

COME-CLEAN HANDS

Nonstick cooking spray is a gadget designed for the kitchen. But Linda Harris of Fulton, Kentucky, has turned it into a gardener's aid. "Squirt your hands with nonstick cooking spray before you go out to garden. It will make your hands easier to wash up, and even helps keep them cleaner inside garden gloves," says Harris.

ON HAND: 5-gallon plastic buckets, an old garden hose, and duct tape

TURN THEM INTO: Hand-friendly handles

HOW TO DO IT: Save your hands from the wrath of old bucket handles. When a bucket handle cracks and falls off, replace it with short sections of old garden hose, wrapped with duct tape. The hose gives your hands a bit of extra cushion, and the duct tape prevents the hose handles from sliding.

ALL SOAPED UP

Tired of having to traipse into the house to scrub off gardening grime? Well, traipse no more. Bea Kline of Fort Washington, Pennsylvania, created an outdoor soap station using a cake of soap and an old panty-hose leg—a low-tech soap on a rope! Simply drop the soap to the toe, tie off the end, and hang it near the hose. Now you can wash up right. The soap stays put and air-dries easily.

"Bubby's" Gloves

How many times have you worked in the garden with gloves on and then pulled them off momentarily because you needed to work with bare hands? Of course, you forget to put them back on, and later lose them in the wheelbarrow or bury them in compost. For you, there are "Bubby," or "old country," gloves. These gloves either have no index finger (or no fingers at all) or a slit at the base of the thumb and index finger so you can have easy access to two digits without needing to remove (and lose) your gloves.

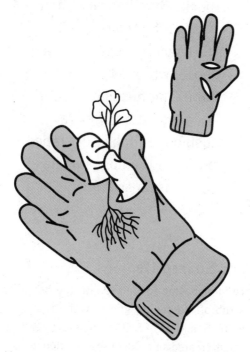

Handy slits at the base of a glove's thumb and index finger make it easier for you to do more detailed work in your garden.

Hammer Out the Best of Black Walnuts

Black walnut nutmeats are delicious, but the nuts are notoriously hard to crack, and the force needed to break the shell often pulverizes the nut meat as well, leading to painstaking work to remove bits of shell from the goodies. Walnut lover Marie Bedics of Whitehall, Pennsylvania, who grew up smashing black walnuts between two rocks, learned a trick years ago that she still uses today, with a little more finesse.

Positioning the nut is what counts most, says Bedics. "Black walnuts are easiest to crack if you hold them pointy end down and whack them on the flatter stem end of the nut," she asserts. "The shell splits open that way to expose the biggest possible pieces of nut meat, so you don't end up with a handful of crumbs."

Bedics still uses a sturdy rock to support the nut for cracking, but nowadays she hits them with a hammer to break the shell. "I've tried nutcrackers," she says, "but with a little practice to get the amount of force just right, a hammer works much better."

Beverage Bowl

Felder Rushing of Jackson, Mississippi, is never without a cold drink while gardening, thanks to the beverage spear he created. Rushing welded a shallow bowl to the top of a 4-foot-long metal rod. He sticks the rod in the ground wherever he's working in the garden and puts a glass or can with his drink of choice in the bowl, where it's in no danger of being knocked over. "Because I welded a metal flower to the bowl, I always think, 'Hey, this bud's for *me!*'" says Rushing.

Save Your Back with a Dustpan "Shovel"

When you have a big pile of soil to move, try this dustpan trick. "I've found that a dustpan is a lot easier to use than a shovel," confesses garden writer Tina James of Reisterstown, Maryland. "I kneel on a kneeling pad, dig in with the dustpan, and fill my wheelbarrow or buckets from that position. It may look a little silly, but who cares when you can get out of bed without groaning the next day!"

Turn Your Hoe into a Ruler

For accurate measurements without carrying a yardstick, use an indelible marker to transfer the markings from a ruler onto the wooden handle of your favorite hoe, rake, or trowel. For a longer-lasting guide, carve the markings into the handle with a whittling knife.

Recycle It!

On hand: An old coal shovel (with a flat, not rounded, blade)

Turn it into: A heavy container mover

How to do it: Simply stick the shovel's blade under the container, and then pull the container like a sled.

Irrigating and Feeding Devices

A plant is a plant is a plant. Right? Well, not quite. How much water a plant is given can make all the difference in the world. You can use soda bottles, PVC, milk jugs, old T-shirts, and much more to keep your house and garden plants healthy and hydrated. In the next few pages, you'll find out *how*.

LOW-TECH IRRIGATION

Deliver water right to the spot it's needed with a low-tech individual watering system made from a milk jug. To get started, wash out a 1-gallon plastic milk jug and make a pin prick or two in the bottom. You want a small enough hole to have a drip, not a steady stream.

Then bury the milk jug up to its neck next to the plant it will irrigate. This works especially well with tomatoes, which like generous, steady amounts of water deep down.

You can also use it to deliver liquid fertilizer or compost tea. Be sure to strain the tea well first.

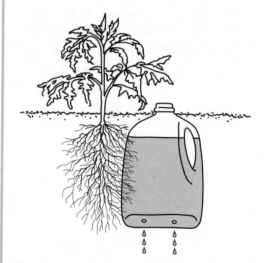

GIVE TOMATOES THE DEEP WATERING THEY LOVE WITH A LOW-TECH MILK-JUG IRRIGATION SYSTEM.

QUICK FIX WITH WICKS

If you live in a rainy climate, you know excess moisture can be a problem, particularly if you enjoy growing plants in containers. Heavy rains are certainly nothing new to Andres Mejides—his certified organic farm in Homestead, Florida, receives periodic drenchings throughout the season—but he found that his collection of unusual plants growing in unusual containers often became waterlogged. Some of his containers drained slowly, while others, such as an old tea kettle, didn't drain at all. Mejides solved this problem using kerosene lamp wicking, which you can find in most hardware stores. He placed one end in a pot that needed draining and let the other end trail down to the ground or into a larger potted plant that drained well. Now he doesn't have to constantly tip the dozens of pots after a big rain. "Plus," he says, "the mosquitoes have fewer places to breed."

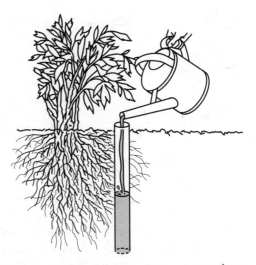

WATER DIRECTLY TO PLANT ROOTS (AND CONSERVE WATER IN THE PROCESS) USING A PIECE OF PVC PIPE.

WATER NOT WASTED

Many plants thrive when given thorough waterings that encourage deep, strong roots. But that takes time and lots of water. Sally Cummings of Albany, New York, has come up with a simple solution. When planting, she buries one end of a PVC pipe next to the plant. She uses slender pipe for perennials and buries 6 to 12 inches of the pipe below ground. For shrubs she uses wider pipe and sinks them deeper into the ground—a foot or more. Just an inch or two needs to remain above ground to ensure it doesn't get covered or clogged with mulch.

"Every time I water I place the hose (or watering can) in the tube and give the plant a good drink. Water goes directly to the roots and isn't wasted by evaporation from the surface of the ground," Cummings says. "This system is especially useful during a drought when you aren't allowed to use hoses or sprinklers," she adds.

GARDEN NURSE

You can tend to tender annuals or forlorn perennials that need some TLC without sacrificing a lot of your time or attention. Donna Armstrong of Harleysville, Pennsylvania, shares her simple plant-nursing secret. "I use a 3-inch-wide strip of cotton fabric for a wick to create a slow drip watering system. T-shirt strips work great."

Here's how Armstrong's system works. Fill a plastic jug with water, then roll the cotton into a wick and place one end in the jug. Tamp the other end of the fabric into the soil at the base of the plant that needs special attention. The water siphons through the wick, providing a gentle water supply.

EASY AUTOMATIC WATERER

This literally cool idea comes from Geraldine Braswell who gardens in Fulton, Kentucky. One spring she planted two rather large new trees.

(continued on page 22)

Build It!

A BASIC BRAMBLE DRIP LINE

Growing your own small fruits like raspberries and blackberries can offer tremendously tasty results, but the plants won't produce big, juicy berries unless they get a regular supply of water. In the Tennessee Valley, gardener Barbara Pleasant planted her brambles in a 50-foot-long row and devised a permanent drip irrigation line to supply the plants with water. "I used plain old PVC pipe because it's cheap, and because it will last for years if it's protected from sun." To take care of the sun problem, Pleasant mulches her berries and the drip line with 3 inches of wheat straw. You can adapt Pleasant's technique for any length row.

Materials

1/2-inch-diameter PVC, the length of your crop row (sold in 10- and 20-foot lengths)

1/2-inch PVC coupling fittings (as needed to connect lengths of plastic pipe)

PVC pipe cement and primer

1/2-inch-diameter PVC end cap

5/8-inch clamp-type female hose connector

12-inch piece of 5/8-inch garden hose

Adjustable metal hose clamp

Wheat straw or other coarse organic mulch

Dark-colored marking pen

Drill with 1/8-inch bit (A brad-point bit works best because it has a self-starting tip.)

DIRECTIONS

1. If you already have an existing patch of berries, rake back the mulch (and weed while you're at it). If you've just planted a new row of plants, don't spread mulch until you lay out your piping.

2. Lay the PVC pipe down the row, and cement the straight lengths together with coupling fittings to get the full length of the row. Also, cement the end cap in place. Cementing PVC pipe is a two-step procedure: First wet the mating surfaces with a primer, then immediately apply the glue to both parts and press them together. The pipe, couplings, and end cap must be dry for the cement to set properly.

3. Use the marking pen to mark the locations of drip holes. Mark holes at regular 6-inch intervals to water a continuous row of plants. Or, you can plan for holes only at the intervals that will work best to deliver water right at the bases of your plants.

4. Drill the holes. If the bit you're using slides off the pipe before it bites in, poke small indentations at each marked spot with an awl or nail to give the bit a starting point.

5. Install the female hose connector to one end of the garden hose, and attach the other end to the PVC pipe with the hose clamp.

6. Connect the system to a garden hose and turn on the water at very low pressure—less than one-quarter turn of the faucet. Wait a few minutes and check to see that water is dripping out all of the holes.

7. Once you're satisfied that the system is working properly, spread mulch over the hose and around the base of the plants.

8. To water your bramble patch, let the water run for 1 hour, and then check the moisture level in the soil. Brambles are fairly shallow-rooted, but it's a good idea to soak at least the top 6 inches of the soil. If necessary, turn the water back on for more time to complete the job. How often you'll need to water will depend on temperature, humidity, rainfall, and the amount of mulch you use. Rather than watering according to a rigid schedule, check soil moisture every few days, and water whenever the soil is dry from 2 to 6 inches below the surface.

9. At the end of the season, check the line to make sure the holes are facing downward so all the water will drain out because water left inside can crack the pipe if it freezes. You can also disconnect the pipe from the hose section and raise the capped end to fully drain the pipe.

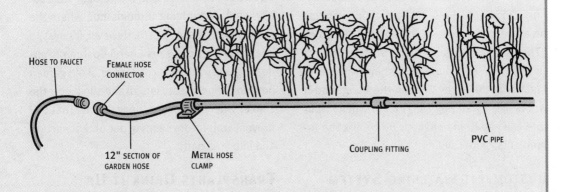

HOSE TO FAUCET

FEMALE HOSE CONNECTOR

12" SECTION OF GARDEN HOSE

METAL HOSE CLAMP

COUPLING FITTING

PVC PIPE

When a drought hit during the summer, she was able to keep her trees well watered throughout the blazingly dry year with minimum fuss—no heavy lifting or toting required! She turned two 5-gallon plastic buckets into a slow-but-sure drip system—one for each tree. Braswell punched a few small holes in the bottom of each bucket with an ice pick. (You could also use an awl.). She then placed the buckets near the tree trunks and over the root-ball area. Braswell kept the bucket waterers filled with the help of a garden hose—no hauling of heavy watering cans. The slow-drip watering enabled her newly planted trees to establish well and quickly in their new landscape. You can also use a bucket waterer to slow-feed flowering trees and shrubs during the spring and summer. Just mix an organic fertilizer into the water of the 5-gallon bucket, and let it slowly soak into the ground around the plants.

Not Your Mother's Watering Can

Milk jugs make the best watering cans for applying manure teas and herbal remedies to plants, says Lisa Ann Haynes of Mahomet, Illinois. "First I put a bung, like the kind you use on a carboy for beer, in the spout," she says. "The hole in the bung is the perfect fit for a tiny spray head I found in the hardware store. I just plug the spray head in the bung, and it works like a watering can, except when I want to, I can cap it and shake it up to mix the ingredients," she says.

Custom-Fit Watering System

You can keep those difficult-to-water areas (such as under the eaves or out of the sprinkler's reach) nicely moist with this customized

sprinkler system developed by Gary Prochaska, a professional gardener in Ames, Iowa.

Prochaska cuts a piece of $\frac{1}{2}$-inch PVC pipe to the length needed. He caps one end of the pipe with a plug and the other with an adapter designed to fit a garden hose. He then drills holes in the PVC with a $\frac{1}{16}$-inch drill bit in a straight line, 2 inches apart. Prochaska attaches a hose and places the PVC wherever he needs to water.

The advantage to this device, Prochaska says, is that he can adjust the flow slightly either by burying the pipe for a slow root soak or putting it on the surface of the soil for a gentle spraying effect.

KEEP THOSE HARD-TO-WATER AREAS FROM DRYING OUT WITH YOUR OWN CUSTOM WATERING SYSTEM.

Don't Get Soaked!

If you use soaker hoses in the garden, you usually wind up trudging through mud where the soaker hose crosses a path. However, it's easy to keep your feet dry, says Cheryl Coston of Fairdealing, Missouri. Just cut a piece of old garden hose to the necessary length and slip it over the soaker where it crosses the walkway. That will prevent water from seeping out of that section and into your path.

Transplants Drink It Up

"After a full day of moving plants around in my garden or setting out new ones, I don't have the energy or the patience to stand

Build It!

DEEP-REACH IRRIGATION BOTTLES

Dry-climate gardeners need to be resourceful to get water to their thirsty crops. Just wetting the surface isn't enough, though; you need to get the water down deep, where the roots are. An organic gardener from Senegal devised this clever way to convert recycled plastic bottles into deep-reaching irrigation bottles that are perfect for squash, melons, tomatoes, or any vegetable planted in hills.

Materials

Narrow-mouthed plastic soda or water bottles (1 or 2 liter)

1 foot length of ¾-inch PVC pipe for each bottle

Durabond PVC adhesive

Utility knife or sturdy scissors

Hacksaw

DIRECTIONS

1. Cut away the bottom of each bottle using a utility knife or scissors.

2. Cut one end of each pipe at a steep angle with a hacksaw, or ask your hardware store clerk to cut it for you.

3. Insert the mouth of the soda bottle into the flat end of a PVC pipe section, or slip the pipe into the mouth of the bottle (whichever works with the bottle you've chosen).

4. Fasten the two parts together with nontoxic Durabond PVC adhesive and let dry.

To use the irrigation bottle, stick the pointed end of the PVC into the soil about 6 inches deep, several inches from the plant. Fill the bottle with water once a day or as often as needed to give plants a deep drink.

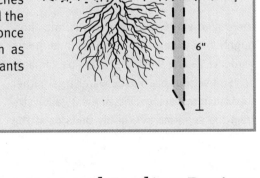

PVC PIPE

6"

ON HAND: Plastic mustard squeeze bottle

TURN IT INTO: A watering device for fragile seedlings

HOW TO DO IT: Clean the mustard bottle in hot soapy water. Fill it with lukewarm to tepid water (70° to 90°F), and screw the top on securely. Squeeze water on soil around seedlings or use to add water to the bottom tray. The small bottle is easy to manipulate around seedling trays (especially those under fluorescent lights) and the flow of water is easy to control.

there and water each one slowly and thoroughly," says environmentalist and home gardener Valerie West of St. Phillips, Indiana.

"So I set out big plastic water jugs, either the kind from water coolers or the 3-gallon size from the supermarket, in my beds or at the base of new trees and shrubs. I punch a few holes near the bottom of the sides of the jug. I can fill the jug in minutes with the hose, and water dribbles out for hours at a slow rate so none is wasted." For the heavy-duty, 5-gallon, water cooler–size jugs, you may need to hammer a nail through the hard plastic to create the holes.

It's easy to delegate the refilling of the water jugs to your kids. They'll welcome a chance to play with the hose, and the task will make them feel like they're a part of making the garden grow.

WATERING THE GREENHOUSE

Susan Cooker of Malvern, Pennsylvania, has an unheated greenhouse, but she makes the most of it, extending her indoor growing season from very early spring through late fall with the help of plastic soda bottles. Susan says the bottles are great for adding both heat and humidity to the air. "It isn't pretty, but it works," she remarks about the many bottles filled two-thirds full with water. Cooker lines the perimeter of her greenhouse with them.

For a handy supply of water, Cooker had gutters installed on the greenhouse roof to funnel rain water into a rain barrel. She then retrofitted an old hose into the draining valve of the barrel so she can easily fill watering cans or buckets from her clean water reserve.

NO-BLEED FEED

"After opening a 5-pound bag of organic fertilizer, I slip it into a plastic grocery bag so the fertilizer won't leak through to the floor or shelf where I store it," says Caroline Whitenack of Doylestown, Pennsylvania.

Although a plastic bag can prevent moisture from getting into the fertilizer bag, you can use a plastic bucket with a lid for even more security. Small critters like mice can chew through a plastic bag and then nibble on your fertilizer. If mice are a potential problem, recycle a food-grade plastic bucket (usually available from restaurants, bakeries, and grocery stores for free or a nominal charge).

EASY RAIN GAUGE

Make your own rain gauge from a straight-sided clear plastic drinking cup (the disposable type is fine) with about 12- to 16-ounce capacity. Using a ruler and measuring from the bottom, mark with a permanent marker at $\frac{1}{2}$-inch increments all the way up the outside of the glass. In a sunny area in the garden (where there are no overhanging trees or branches), set the glass down into the soil (sinking 2 to 3 inches). "After a rain, pull the cup out to read, or insert a ruler down into the cup to measure rainfall," says Linda Harris from Fulton, Kentucky. "This rain gauge will last one or two seasons."

FERTILIZER FAST

If you're tired of lugging watering cans and buckets filled with liquid fertilizer or compost tea to your plants, try this fast watering/fertilizing system developed by Tonya Halberstadt of Ben Wheeler, Texas.

Halberstadt puts a 55-gallon, food-safe drum (she finds hers at flea markets or salvage yards) in her vegetable garden. She punches a hole near the bottom and inserts a piece of PVC fitting, caulking well around the edge of the hole to prevent leakage. Then she

attaches a soaker hose to the PVC and lays it around the vegetable garden. She fills the drum with water from the garden hose and mixes in the fertilizer.

"I've had a real time with fertilizers," Halberstadt says. "I'd do one row but not the next. This way everything gets fertilized at once."

In her large garden Halberstadt also likes to hook up more than one drum to the other to create an even bigger reservoir. To do this, she again punches a hole near the bottom in the side of the original drum as well as in a new drum. She attaches them with a short length of PVC and then caulks again.

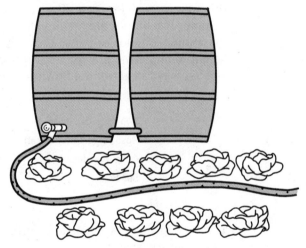

MAKE FERTILIZING AS EASY AS TURNING A SPIGOT WITH A SYSTEM USING LOW-COST, RECYCLED METAL DRUMS.

EASY INDOOR WATERING

Nancy Engel, who gardens in Cold Spring, New York, has an extensive array of houseplants that used to be a bear to water. But not anymore since her husband devised an indoor-watering system. He screwed a quick-release

Build It!

55-GALLON DRUM WATERING SYSTEM

Industrial 55-gallon drums are inexpensive and easy to find and hold almost as much water as a 100-square-foot garden needs in a week. Making a watering reservoir out of one of these drums isn't hard, and can sure save on time and muscle power devoted to hauling water. When buying or recycling drums for your garden, use only those that have held fruit juices or other nontoxic substances.

To make garden irrigation easier, use a "passive" 55-gallon drum watering system, recommended by Charles Young of Philadelphia's Pennsylvania State Urban Gardening Program. The system uses gravity to move the water instead of a pump. Two barrels are required for this system, with one barrel sunk slightly into the ground. The lower barrel provides a base for the second barrel giving needed height for effective, gravity-fed irrigation. Installing a faucet in the upper barrel is an easy way to control the flow of water to your garden.

Materials

Two 55-gallon drums

Hose bib (exterior faucet)

Old garden hose

Spade

Electric drill with specialty bit or metal-cutting hole saw

Welding kit

DIRECTIONS

1. Using a spade, dig a hole 18 to 24 inches deep, and wide enough to receive a drum. Level the bottom of the hole.

2. Put one drum in the hole, then backfill around the edge of the drum, and tamp the soil.

male coupler onto each of the upstairs and downstairs faucets. Then he screwed together two 10-foot lengths of $1/2$-inch-diameter plastic hose, screwed a female coupler onto one end of the hose, and snapped that end onto the male coupler on the downstairs

faucet. He made the same setup for the upstairs faucet.

Engel can use her hoses as is by simply attaching a quick-connect system that has an on-off switch, or she can customize her watering by using either of two other attach-

3. Using a metal-cutting hole saw or a drill with a specialty bit, make a 1-inch hole in the side of the other drum, 1 to 3 inches from its bottom edge.

4. Push the long threaded end of the exterior faucet (plumbing suppliers call it a hose bib) into the hole. Use your welding kit to weld the faucet threads to the inside of the drum.

5. Position the drum on top of the sunken drum, making sure they nestle together securely.

6. Fill top drum with water.

7. Once you attach a hose to the drum's faucet, you're ready to have a well-watered garden.

One variation on this watering system involves connecting raised drums with spigots to drip irrigation hoses to create a gravity-powered irrigation drip system. Or, instead of irrigating your plants directly from a drum, you can feed water from a raised drum to a water reservoir and then connect gravity-fed, drip-irrigation garden hoses to the reservoir. Whatever technique you decide to use, your garden will benefit from a continuous and reliable source of water.

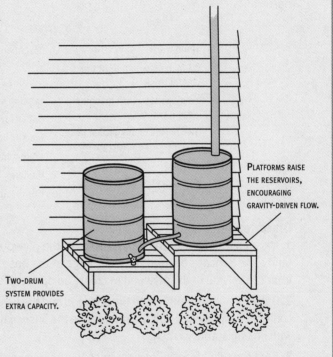

PLATFORMS RAISE THE RESERVOIRS, ENCOURAGING GRAVITY-DRIVEN FLOW.

TWO-DRUM SYSTEM PROVIDES EXTRA CAPACITY.

ments—a plastic hose nozzle with twist shut-off or a watering wand for window boxes.

"From the upstairs sink, I can reach plants in two bedrooms and all of my second-story window boxes," Engel says. "The downstairs connection allows me to get from the front to the back of my house as well as from one end to the other to water plants in every room. And the on-off switch allows me to keep the faucet turned on, but without dripping water on the floor as I move from plant to plant."

Build It!

CLARK PARK "WATER ON WHEELS"

Lewis Mellman, a tree tender from Clark Park in west Philadelphia, built this contraption for watering trees when he had little or no access to a hose. He strapped a 35-gallon rectangular trash can to a hand truck and then mounted a beer tap at the bottom.

Materials

- Hand truck
- ¾-inch plywood, to fit the hand truck
- Four ¼ × 1½-inch machine bolts and nuts
- Two pieces of old garden hose, same length as the plywood
- 12 nails
- PVC faucet and flange bolt
- 35-gallon rectangular plastic trash can
- Silicone caulk
- Lashing straps or rope
- Saber saw
- Electric drill with ⁵⁄₁₆-inch bit
- Adjustable wrench
- Hammer
- Utility knife

DIRECTIONS

1. Measure the base of the hand truck. Cut the plywood to size with a saber saw so it extends 2 to 3 inches beyond the front edge of the base. Also, cut a U-shaped notch in the front center side of the plywood to create an opening for a faucet.

2. Drill four holes through both the plywood and the base of the hand truck—one near each corner of the plywood. Bolt the plywood to the base of the hand truck, and tighten the bolts with an adjustable wrench.

3. Split the two pieces of garden hose lengthwise, and nail the pieces to the front of the plywood to create bumpers on either side of the U-shaped notch.

4. Install the PVC faucet in the front bottom of the trash can so that when the can is placed on the base of the hand truck and liquid runs from the faucet, the liquid will flow through the plywood's U-shaped notch. To do this, cut a round hole in the trash can with a utility knife and insert the threaded end of the faucet into the hole from the outside of the can.

Apply a generous bead of silicone caulk to the base of the threads, and then connect and tighten the flange bolt to the faucet threads. Allow the silicone to dry overnight before filling the can with water.

5. Strap or tie the trash can to the hand truck so that the faucet hangs over the plywood's U-shaped notch.

6. Fill the trash can half-full with water. To use your super-size watering can on wheels, guide it up to the base of each tree, open the faucet, and water generously.

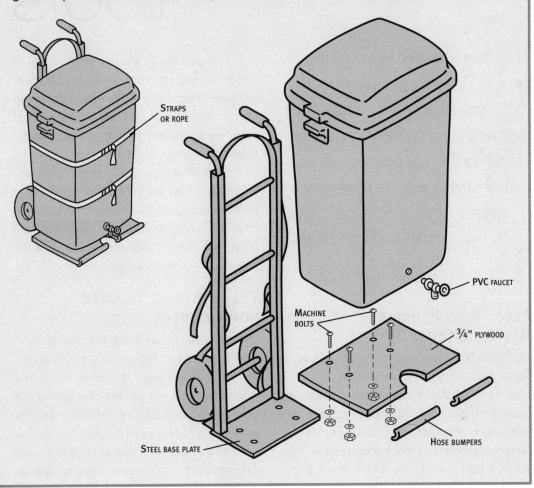

STRAPS OR ROPE

PVC FAUCET

MACHINE BOLTS

3/4" PLYWOOD

HOSE BUMPERS

STEEL BASE PLATE

Lawn and Landscape Tools

Don't be overwhelmed by your lawn or landscape. There are plenty of creative ways that you can make your maintenance plan easier to handle. The following tips will provide you with time-saving ways to edge, fence, clean up, and build raised beds, walkways, and walls.

FENCE-POST POUNDER BEATS A HAMMER

One of the best things about using metal posts for garden fencing or trellising is that you don't have to dig holes for the posts. However, pounding the posts into the ground is no easy job either. Pennsylvania market gardener Melanie DeVault finds that the best tool for the job is a post pounder or driver. "I'm 5 foot, 2 inches tall, and I just don't have the reach or strength to drive a post into the ground with any kind of hammer," DeVault explains.

A post pounder is a 2-foot-long section of 3-inch pipe with a metal cap on one end. To use it, you slide the pounder over the top of the post, and lean the post and pounder upright. Then lift and drop the post pounder. The impact of the pounder cap hitting the post drives it into the ground.

Post pounders are available at many hardware stores, farm and garden centers, and even some building-supply centers. You can also have one custom-made at a local machine shop—ask them to weld a steel disk onto the end of a 2-foot section of pipe.

TURN A STRING TRIMMER INTO AN EDGER

String trimmers have quickly become a must-have tool for lawn and property maintenance. And sure, they're great for cutting weeds and grass, but that's not all they can do! You can turn almost any trimmer into a lawn-and-garden edger simply by turning the cutting head 90 degrees (so it's on its side) and using a steady hand to guide the rotating string head slightly above the ground.

"Gas-powered edgers work best," says Mike Ferrara, a gardener from the Minneapolis area, "because they can handle thicker line in their spools." Ferrara says a cord called "star line" (it's actually molded into the shape of a star) works great for this purpose because it cuts through thick vegetation and lasts a long time. It's also a good idea to use a trimmer that has a standard tap-and-feed head, which means that when the nylon line wears away, you simply tap the head on the ground to feed out a predetermined length of line.

When used as an edger, the star line will leave a nice, thick trench—ideal for tidying up around your raised beds and your sidewalks. When using your string trimmer/edger, it's important to wear safety goggles and leather gloves at all times and to make sure the stone guard is correctly attached to your trimmer.

TURNING THE CUTTING HEAD ON YOUR STRING TRIMMER GIVES YOU AN INSTANT EDGER.

ON HAND: An old vinyl rug runner

TURN IT INTO: Sunken edging strips

HOW TO DO IT: Using a utility knife, cut the runner into strips about 6 inches wide and sink them into the ground around a garden bed. They'll keep roots from moving into the lawn or path and will also help deter underground burrowers such as moles. (You can also use the vinyl strips around individual plants to deter cutworms.) If the ground is soft, simply sink the strips into the ground. If the soil is hard packed, dig a slim trench, place the strips in the trench, and then refill the trench with soil.

RHODODENDRON FENCING

Rhododendrons tend to get big in Oregon, and sometimes they need a hearty pruning. A landscape architect by training, Rodney Wojtanik

Build It!

SNAPPY STEPPING-STONES

Stepping-stones are a must for large garden beds so you can maneuver your way around the plants without tamping down the soil. But they can be expensive to buy. "Make your own and make them as pretty as you like," says Linda Harris of Fulton, Kentucky. "Press shells, pretty pebbles, or large leaves into the concrete after pouring. Or scratch in your own choice of names, dates, words, handprints, footprints, paw-prints, or drawings after pouring." Ask for a bucket at your grocery store, bakery, or local restaurant. They're usually willing to give them away for free. This idea came from a lady in Martin, Tennessee, that I met at a garden open house," says Harris. "It was such a neat idea that I want to pass it along."

Materials

5-gallon plastic bucket with straight sides	Band saw or sharp X-Acto knife
60-pound bag of concrete mix	Plastic drop cloth
Wooden stirring paddle	Old pencil for drawing, or decorative shells, leaves, or pebbles
Tape measure or ruler	

DIRECTIONS

1. Measure the height of the bucket and divide by 5. Then mark that measurement (about 3 inches) down the side of the bucket. Repeat, making three more marks at the same interval.

2. Saw or cut through the bucket crosswise at each of the marked intervals to make five bands or stepping-stone

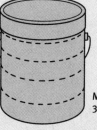

MEASURE AT 3" INTERVALS.

knows how to cut them back, and he also knows how to use all those prunings in a pro-ductive way. Wojtanik fenced in his wife's herb bed with his rhododendron trimmings. He pushed sturdier straight pieces into the ground to serve as uprights and then used longer, thinner branches as the "rails." He ties the pieces together with steel wire, which quickly rusts and becomes nearly invisible.

ANOTHER STEPPING-STONE TIP

There's more than one option for forming "Snappy Stepping-Stones" as described above. You can also make forms for stepping-stones in your garden from Sonotube, those sturdy cardboard tubes that are sold for pouring concrete footings; they're available at most home centers. Using a hacksaw, cut the Sono-tube into sections as thick as you want your molds. The top of the bucket with the handle attached is one mold. The bucket bottom is also a mold; you can keep the bottom intact or remove it.

3. Lay the bucket circles on a flat surface covered with a plastic drop cloth.

4. Mix concrete as directed on the package, and pour it into your circle molds. A 60-pound bag will yield enough concrete to pour five stepping-stones that are each a little more than 1 inch thick.

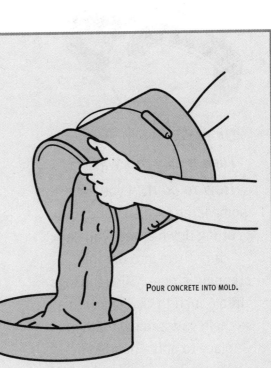

POUR CONCRETE INTO MOLD.

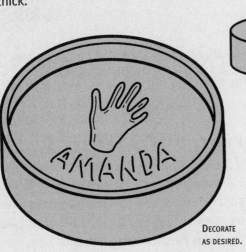

DECORATE
AS DESIRED.

5. Level the surfaces, and decorate as desired, using an old pencil or decorative stones to make a pattern or design.

6. When the concrete is set, push your new stepping-stones out of the molds. Save your molds for the next pouring.

stepping-stones to be. Lay the circular forms on the ground where you want the stones. Mix concrete according to the instructions on the bag, and fill the forms. Allow the concrete to set until nearly dry, then cut and peel off the cardboard Sonotube.

If you plan to decorate the stones with a design or imprint, be sure to do so before the concrete is thoroughly dry.

REUSED CONCRETE

Wherever concrete pavements are being replaced, you'll see dump trucks full of the old broken-up concrete headed to a landfill. Fred Conrad, the community garden coordinator for the Atlanta Food Bank, "saw gold in them-there trucks" and started salvaging the common refuse for garden walls and raised beds. Calling his material "recrete," Conrad collects old

ON HAND: Tree trunk slabs
TURN THEM INTO: Walkway
HOW TO DO IT: If you have some large logs on hand from cutting down a tree, you can turn them into organic stepping-stones. Slice the logs into 6-inch-thick disks with a chain saw and lay them in place to add a handsome rustic touch to your landscape!

new one; it's just that he likes it that way! Bray found that by removing the bent or damaged side tines from his old leaf rake, he can create the perfect recycled tool for removing leaves and other debris that gets caught between the densely planted hostas and daylilies at his Yardley, Pennsylvania, home.

TO MAKE YOUR OWN MINI RAKE, SIMPLY USE TIN SNIPS OR HEAVY SHEARS TO CUT OFF ALL BUT FOUR OR FIVE OF THE CENTER TINES FROM AN OLD LEAF RAKE.

broken slabs from areas where sidewalk, driveway, or road work is being done. The pieces are usually fairly uniform in thickness and flat on two or three surfaces, making them easy to dry-stack into a garden wall. You can also set them on one side to create a vertical wall for a raised bed. Conrad finds recrete ideal for many reasons. "It's considerably lighter than stone, it doesn't leach anything toxic like treated wood does, and its rough edges lend a natural look to your garden—especially in wet climates where the recrete gets nice and mossy."

BREAK A RAKE

When Jim Bray cleans out the six perennial beds on his 1-acre lot, he prefers to use a broken rake. It isn't because he can't afford a

PRETTY BRANCH SPREADERS

If Darlene White invites you to take a look at her pot plant, don't get nervous. This British Columbia garden writer has simply devised an elegant way to spread the branches of her pear tree using hanging terra-cotta pots!

Many shade and fruit trees—pears in particular—tend to hold their branches too tightly together as they grow, and gardeners have traditionally hung lead weights on the branches to force them to grow out and not up. White, however, wanted something a little prettier to gaze at during the growing months.

In the spring, she gathered about 2 dozen old terra-cotta pots all the same general size (usually about 6 to 7 inches wide). She tied one end of a 15-inch piece of fishing line around a long nail and threaded the other end through the drainage hole. The pot hung upside down like a bell, making it easy to attach it to a branch she wanted to spread. To adjust how much the branch will spread, simply move the weight in or out from the tree trunk. Add more pots until all the limbs that you want to spread have a pot attached.

White keeps the amount of line between the pot bottom and branch to about 5 inches, to keep the pots from smacking each other in the breeze. The limbs should be settled into their new growth pattern by the end of the growing season, so remove the pots before any unexpected early snowfall adds too much weight and snaps the branches.

TURN UNUSED CLAY POTS INTO ATTRACTIVE BRANCH SPREADERS FOR FRUIT OR SHADE TREES. THEY MAKE AN INTERESTING GARDEN ACCENT, TOO!

ON HAND: Scrap piece of ¼-inch wire mesh

TURN IT INTO: A stepping "stone" near a water spigot

HOW TO DO IT: Place a square of recycled ¼-inch wire mesh on the soil or mulch surface under a water spigot. The mesh prevents puddling, allowing water to pass through it and giving you a firm, clean place to step.

PIPE DREAMS

It's fun to decorate your garden with lanterns and other ornaments, but it isn't much fun to keep straightening them up when soggy soil allows their stakes to keel over. Living in rainy Seattle, garden writer and consultant Madeleine Wilde knows that all too well! She solved her problem by installing a short section of galvanized or PVC pipe into the ground as a permanent mounting hole for each ornament. To use this great idea in your own garden, simply choose the appropriate diameter of pipe and, with a heavy hammer, pound it in flush or slightly lower than the ground level to facili-

tate mowing. Madeleine also finds a set of these pipe supports useful for positioning her spiked sprinkler during those rare dry spells.

A QUICKER PICKER UPPER

There's no question that sweet gum (*Liquidambar styraciflua*) trees are gorgeous, especially in autumn. But if you've ever had them in your landscape, you know that they have a down side: Their hard, spiky fruits are a nuisance when they fall to the lawn or sidewalk. Picking them up is a difficult, time-consuming, and sometimes even painful job. But Wendy Goldberg of Wilmington, Delaware, invented an ingenious sweet-gum-ball picker upper. "I took a stick (actually a hollow, dried Jerusalem artichoke stem because it's lighter than wood) and tied polyester batting (the kind used in pillows) to the end," she ex-

plains. Goldberg walks around the yard with her picker upper and just touches the end to the fallen fruit. The sweet gum balls stick to the batting, enabling her to pick them up without bending over. From there, it's a simple matter to pick off the sweet gum balls and drop them in a bucket for disposal later.

LITTER GRABBER

Tired of jumping off your lawn tractor to pick up debris that blocks your path? Try this ingenious trash grabber devised by Carolyn Roof, Master Gardener and garden columnist for the *Paducah Sun* newspaper, Paducah, Kentucky. Take an old wooden handle from a broom, rake, or other tool, and saw it off to a comfortable length for you. Hammer three finishing nails into one end, and then take it with you when you mow by tractor. "Using this trash grabber is a lot simpler than getting off the tractor, picking up litter, and having to restart the tractor," says Roof. "There's some litter I don't want to pick up by hand. And this tool works for almost everything except glass. The nails will even puncture and pick up aluminum cans."

MOWING METER

What's the worst thing you can do to your lawn? Cut off too much at once. The golden rule of mowing says you should never remove more than one-third of a grass blade at any one time. But most of us don't mow according to the needs of the grass. That's why Warren Schultz of Essex Junction, Vermont, made a simple mowing meter that tells him when he should crank up the mower.

His lawn is made of tall fescue, which shouldn't be cut shorter than 3 inches. To make a measuring stick, he started with an 8-inch-long, 1 × 1-inch stake with a point at one end. He painted the bottom 2 inches brown, the next 3 inches green, the next 1½ inches yellow, and the rest red. Then he sank the brown section into the ground to one side of his lawn. When the height of the grass reaches the top of the green band, he knows it has reached its ideal height. As it grows into the yellow area, he knows it's time to mow it back down to the top of the green band. If the blades ever reach into the red area, he knows that he has let the grass grow too tall and that he needs to make a series of cuts to gradually trim it back down to the ideal height.

Put Horsepower to Work

"I loved the big old forsythia bush that we inherited when we bought our farmhouse," says home gardener Linda Howard of Evansville, Indiana. "But it was in the wrong place—it blocked my view from the kitchen window so I couldn't see the garden beyond it."

Linda and her husband, Rick, decided to move the large shrub to a new site, but after 2 days of digging, it was still anchored like a buried boulder and gave no signs of budging. That's when she decided to turn to a mechanical aid—their small pickup truck. "I wrapped the bottom of the stems in burlap and fastened a strong rope around them. We tied the rope to the truck, and I stayed with the bush while Rick began to gently pull with the truck. I couldn't believe how easily the truck pulled it out—those big roots I had tried to dig and then tried to cut through came loose right away."

Rick and Linda dragged the forsythia to its new home and then settled it in place. It recovered quickly and blooms cheerfully each spring

On hand: Popsicle stick

Turn it into: Engine maintenance tool

How to do it: Keep your air-cooled engines running cool by making sure the fins around the cylinder are free from dirt and debris. A Popsicle stick works great for this job: Simply sharpen one end into a point to get stubborn bits of grass out of the fins.

near the corner of the driveway. Linda reports she's planning to use pickup power to pull out a volunteer mulberry tree that she wants to move to a better spot and maybe a few other overgrown heirloom shrubs.

Quick Mower Cleanup

Environmentalist Valerie West of St. Phillips, Indiana, counts on her trusty, heavy-duty screwdriver "whenever anything needs prying, poking, digging," or for any other small-scale jobs where leverage counts. But her favorite use of this perfect, simple tool is for cleaning her lawn mower. "You can slide the screwdriver under the caked-on grass and lift off big chunks," she says. For safety's sake, always securely disconnect the spark plug wire and be sure the gas tank is empty before you do this.

A plain-tip screwdriver with a long, stout shaft also comes in handy for separating and lifting seedlings, particularly those of deep-rooted plants such as young trees or Oriental poppies and other tap-rooted perennials. And if you misplace your dandelion digger, use a trusty screwdriver to lift out tough weeds from the lawn and walks.

MAKE A FENCE MORE FRIENDLY

"A high wood fence was a necessity around my yard because of my unruly dogs and my need for privacy," says Sally Roth, author of *Attracting Birds to Your Backyard*, "but once the fence was up, it really looked forbidding. I like my neighbors, and I like a yard that looks welcoming from the street, so I decided to make the outside walls of the fence just as appealing as the inside.

"Sweet autumn clematis (*Clematis terniflora*) and virgin's bower (*C. virginiana*) pop up everywhere in my yard, thanks to the birds who drop the seeds, so I transplanted every seedling I could find, spacing them about 2 feet apart along the outside of the fence. The problem is, clematis clings by winding the stems of its leaves around a support, but the solid wood face of my fence didn't give them any place to get a grip. So I bought 100 feet of green vinyl-coated 3-foot-high wire fencing and stapled it the long way to the outside of the fence, starting about 2 feet above the bottom of the fence.

"These vines grow like lightning, and within 2 weeks they had reached the wire. They swarmed over it, covering it so thickly I now have a living wall of greenery instead of bare boards. Soon the vines will be draping themselves along the top of the fence, and when summer arrives, they'll be crowning it with soft white flowers that will make my yard smell terrific. When the flowers ripen into fluffy seed heads in fall, my birds will have a banquet right through winter."

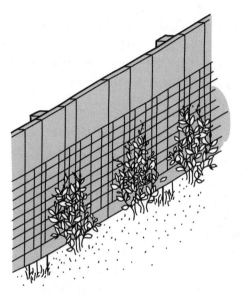

A SOLID WOOD FENCE IS MUCH MORE NEIGHBORLY WHEN YOU COVER IT WITH PRETTY CLIMBING VINES.

CONSIDER ALL THE ANGLES

"If it weren't for my camera," says Gretel Hartman of the Boston area, "my garden wouldn't look half as good as I like to think it does!" Designing a garden before planting it can be an acquired skill, so Hartman depends on her camera to show her what works and what doesn't.

"When I'm in my garden, I get so involved looking at my plants," she says, "that I can't even tell whether the overall design works. So

I make it a point to snap a roll of film at least once a month, from all angles.

"It's amazing how much difference it makes looking at a picture, rather than looking at the real thing. I can tell right away when a tree or shrub is in the wrong spot, and I can see where the perennial garden looks bare of color."

Hartman files away the photos, month by month, for a record of her garden year. "I like to pull them out in the dead of winter," she says, "first, so I don't lose hope of spring, and second, so I can start thinking about any changes I want to make in the coming year. It's a good way to remind myself of what I need to shop for, too—more of those pink iris, or maybe a weeping cherry for the corner of the garden. . . . "

ROCK HOUND TO THE RESCUE

A rocky garden led garden photographer Rick Mark of Vancouver, Washington, to find a better tool for prying out rocks. It was a Pennsylvania garden where Mark discovered how well a rock hammer works for loosening rocks.

"My family are rock hounds," he says, "and we had a few strong rock hammers lying around. They're made for heavier work than a carpenter's hammer, and they have a head that's designed for levering out rocks." The long, curved piece on the back of the head slides easily under rocks to get a grip, and the strong handle stands up to mini-crowbar work much better than any other tool. The handle slides into the hammer loop on carpenter jeans, keeping the tool handy while gardening.

Mark bought his rock hammer at a lapidary supply shop. Most hardware stores will carry a similar tool, though they may call it a brick mason's hammer.

LIGHT UP YOUR PATH

An easy, inexpensive way to add evening light involves large glass containers, explains Melinda Rizzo, who gardens in Quakertown, Pennsylvania. Mayonnaise jars as well as industrial-strength pickle and hot pepper jars work great. "The bigger the better!" says Rizzo. Soak off the labels and rinse the jars clean. Pour 2 to 3 inches of sand in the jar, then insert a white pillar candle. Use these inexpensive garden lights in the garden at night, to line a brick path, or simply grouped by your favorite garden resting place.

ON HAND: Old swingset

TURN IT INTO: Hammock frame

HOW TO DO IT: Strip all the play equipment off of the A-frame. Spray paint it a subtle color like brown or dark green, and use it to support a hammock in your garden. Recycle the poles from the teeter-totter feature to use as a bean teepee. Wrap them with wire mesh for the vines to twine around.

Build It!

THE SHRUB "CLUB"

"Each time we bought new shrubs and planted them in our whiskey barrels, they'd be stolen overnight," says Anna Maria Vona, who lives and gardens in south Philadelphia. She and her neighbors came up with some effective ways to protect their plants. This "shrub cable," devised by Joe Procaccini to foil the "jerk-and-run thief," is like the antitheft club device you lock onto your steering wheel to foil a car thief.

Materials

Half whiskey barrel or planter

1-inch-diameter threaded eyebolt and nut

2 large flat washers to fit bolt

4-foot length of ¼-inch or ⅜-inch braided cable

Potted shrub or tree

Soil mix

Lightweight fill (optional)

Electric drill and ½-inch bit

DIRECTIONS

1. Drill a ½-inch hole in the bottom of the whiskey barrel, and insert a threaded eyebolt with a washer on both sides of the bottom. Screw on the nut. (If the bottom of the planter rests too close to the ground, mount the eyebolt through the side, just above the bottom.)

2. Fasten one end of the braided cable onto the eyebolt by twisting the end of the cable around itself like a piece of picture frame wire.

3. If desired, put a layer of lightweight fill material in the bottom of the barrel.

4. Remove the shrub or tree from the nursery pot and position it in the planter so it will grow at the same level that it was growing in the nursery pot. Add soil mix to the planter as needed until the plant is at the right height.

5. Wrap the loose end of the braided cable around the trunk of the shrub or tree just above the rootball. Make a loop with enough slack for future growth, and fasten the cable by again twisting it around itself.

6. Finish filling the planter with soil mix. Be sure to bury the braided cable as much as possible in the soil mix so it isn't easy to see.

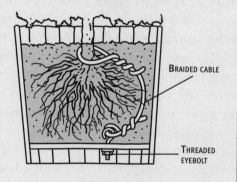

BRAIDED CABLE

THREADED EYEBOLT

Build It!

CUSTOM-MADE POND CLEANER

Ed Bender of Carlsbad, California, has discovered several garden uses for restaurant bus tubs. "They're very handy for carrying things—such as mulch—from one part of the yard to another and they're pretty sturdy," says Bender. However, the best use of all for these tubs may be for cleaning a garden pond. Bender needed a cleaning contraption that would eliminate the problem of ending up with a soaking wet mess. So he made a self-draining container that allows him to easily empty the contents into his compost pile. The water drains off into the bottom of the bus tub, leaving material in the basket, which he then throws in his compost.

Materials

1-inch-mesh chicken wire
cut into pieces:

15 inches × 21 inches

11 inches × 7 inches

11 inches × 7 inches

One restaurant bus tub,
13 × 17 × 6 inches deep

DIRECTIONS

1. Make a 90-degree bend 5 inches from each end of the large piece of chicken wire to form a U-shape.

2. Make a wire basket by attaching the smaller pieces to the open ends of the U, twisting the wires together and leaving a 2-inch overhang at the base of each end.

3. On each 2-inch overhang, bend the bottom 1 inch upward to form a 1-inch-deep foot on each end of the basket.

4. Place the basket inside the bus tub. You should have 1 inch of free space surrounding the basket.

"Fastening doesn't need to be neat," adds Bender. "Just make sure there aren't loose wire ends to jab you." To use, scoop up pond debris and plop it in the tray, allowing the water to drain through the colander into the bus tub. Lift out colander and empty debris into your compost pile.

"In pond maintenance, I have to remove dead water lily leaves and blossoms, and I can't reach them all from the shore," Bender says. "So I take the bus tub arrangement in the water with me. Because the tub floats, I can pull it around as I walk in the pond."

BUS TUB   CHICKEN MESH WIRE

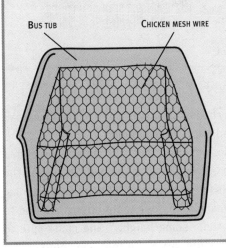

Build-It!

LANTERN DELIGHTS

Buying outdoor lighting from catalogs or garden shops can be expensive. To make her own, Melinda Rizzo, a home gardener in Quakertown, Pennsylvania, uses clean 4- and 6-ounce baby food jars. Once you soak off the labels, fine gauge wire and a small votive candle are all you need to create sparkling evening lights. You can hang these lights on hooks, nails driven into porch beams, or as lanterns on garden poles. Using a citronella votive gives extra bug-off advantages.

Materials

6 to 12 clean baby food jars

Spool of fine-gauge wire
(not plastic coated)

6 to 12 votive candles

6"–10" INCHES OF
WIRE SHOULD EXTEND
ABOVE THE JAR.

DIRECTIONS

1. For each jar, cut a piece of wire 40 to 50 inches long. Vary the lengths so your finished lights can hang at different heights.

2. Bend a wire in half to form a V-shaped handle for the jar. Hold the bent wire over a jar so 6 to 10 inches of the V extends above the jar for hanging. Wrap the rest of the wire around the threads of the jar mouth.

3. Twist each end of the wire around the V-shaped handle to fasten the wire securely. Pull tight.

4. Place a votive candle in the jar, light, and hang.

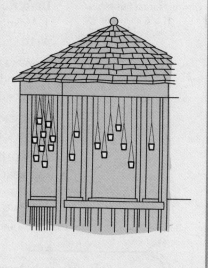

HOMEMADE HOSE GUIDES

An unguided hose can quickly decapitate flowers, but the antique-reproduction hose guides that Pat Hoskins of Evansville, Indiana, had seen in stores and catalogues cost more than she wanted to invest.

"I could see there definitely was value in putting some kind of hose guide at the corners of my beds," she says, "so I decided to use salvaged bricks I had around."

Hoskins used 10 bricks at each corner and each outward bend of the bed. She paired the bricks for stability, and set them on a diagonal "to make them look more interesting and to give them some height." She made sure to use enough bricks so that she could create a curved corner that the hose would run smoothly around.

"My low hose guides work just fine," she reports. "Not once did I whip the head off a tulip or an iris this spring. And the bricks work in another way I hadn't expected: the basket-of-gold and alyssum in the beds spill over that extra little wall like a waterfall."

A DOUBLE CURVED ROW OF BRICKS AT THE CORNERS OF YOUR GARDEN BEDS WILL PREVENT YOUR HOSE FROM STRAYING INTO YOUR PLANTS AND DAMAGING THEM.

KEEP CREEPING PLANTS UNDER CONTROL

Have you ever planted mint or some other fast-creeping plant directly in your garden? If so, you know why traditional wisdom suggests planting them first in a pot, and then sinking the whole pot into the soil to help contain the spreading roots. Sometimes, though, the roots still manage to creep out the pot's drainage holes and romp through the garden. Fortunately, Cheryl Coston of Fairdealing, Mis-

ON HAND: Old hose
TURN IT INTO: Blade protectors
HOW TO DO IT: Cut a piece of old rubber or plastic hose the length of your saw blade, garden hoe, or machete, then make a lengthwise slit in the hose. Slip it over the sharp edge of the blade or hoe to save the blade and protect your hand from cuts and scrapes, says Irv Breber of Bensalem, Pennsylvania.

souri, has figured out a way to keep even the most determined roots in place within the pot. "I cut the bottom off the pot and then used a hot glue gun to fasten a scrap of fiberglass screen to the bottom and about 1 inch up the side of the pot before sinking the pot in the soil. The roots will have less of a chance to escape," she advises.

DON'T SAY GOOD NIGHT!

Want to extend your gardening time? Can't get outside until it's almost dark? Try camping or fishing head lamps! Steve Frowine, avid gardener and director of horticulture at Etera Corporation, says these lamps are great for working in the evening. "It's the most romantic time in the garden," he declares. You can easily extend your garden time by working with these lamps after dark. Small lamps are secured around your head with an elastic band. Your neighbors might think you're nuts, but when time is at a premium, this gadget offers you daylight in the dark.

GARDEN RAIN DRUM

"I saw an incredible Tibetan rain drum in a catalog, but it cost more than $200, and I just couldn't justify it in my budget," says Linda Harris of Fulton, Kentucky. "So I made my own—really simply. Although it doesn't have the exotic appearance, it does amplify the sound of rain, and that's very soothing," adds Harris. To make yours, take a 1-gallon or 10-gallon galvanized metal bucket (or even a galvanized washtub) and set it upside down. Press outward any indentations which may be in the bottom. Hammer one of the edges or lips down (1 to 2 inches long) to make an escape route for the excess water to run out. Set your rain drum on a deck (for best acoustic effect) where there are no branches overhanging, and enjoy the sound of raindrops while it rains. When it's sunny, use the bucket for other purposes!

Multipurpose Gadets

In a garden, the possibilities for innovation are endless. Silverware can function as weeding tools, ironing boards as potting benches, shower curtains as planting totes. Below, read about "Versatile Wire Arches" or learn how to "Slide It in a Saucer" — you'll soon be eager to find new ways to use old things.

GARDEN TABLEWARE

"Odd pieces of tableware from garage sales are great garden tools," says Alabama gardener Barbara Pleasant. She uses a table fork for weeding, keeps a butter knife on her potting table for gently prying plants out of containers with roots intact, and wields a grapefruit spoon to tease apart matted roots when repotting houseplants. "A big serving spoon is also great for moving volunteer seedlings to better locations," Pleasant says.

ROLL OUT THE BARREL

"At Pheasant Hill Farm, we use old plastic barrels, cut in half, as huge vegetable trugs and even weed sleds," says market gardener Melanie DeVault. The barrels — which originally held pickles, apple juice concentrate, or vinegar — cost just $10 each. Husband George cuts them in half lengthwise with a saber saw. They're used for soaking carrots and radishes in icy well water to clean and freshen them and as storage containers. For hauling spent crops when it's time to clean out the garden, the DeVaults attach a rope handle through holes at either end of the half-barrels and easily slide the garden waste along the rows. "The barrels are easier to use than wheelbarrows," says DeVault. "Be creative — any rounded-bottom plastic item can work."

VERSATILE WIRE ARCHES

"The most indispensable items in my garden are sections of 5-foot-tall wire mesh fencing," reports Barbara Pleasant, who grows vegetables year-round in her Alabama garden. Many varieties of fence will work, including the mesh used for reinforcing concrete. Pleasant finds that sections about 7 feet long work best. "In winter I use them as support arches for plastic-covered grow tunnels because they stand up well to wind and occasional ice. In spring, the arches by themselves keep dogs and deer out of newly planted beds, and I also set up one of them covered with well-ventilated plastic to form my version of a coldframe," Pleasant says. In the summer, she bends the arches into cylinders, clasping the hooked ends of the wire together, and uses them as tomato cages. Pleasant notes that it's important to anchor the cages well with stakes because they can blow over when they're top-heavy with tomatoes. When summer ends and it's time to clean up the garden, Pleasant puts the tomato cages to work as temporary compost bins.

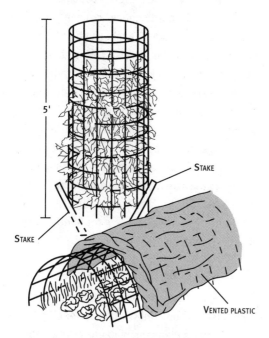

ARCHES MADE FROM WIRE MESH FENCING OR CONCRETE REINFORCING WIRE CAN STAND ERECT TO MAKE A TOMATO CAGE OR ARCH LONGWAYS TO SUPPORT CLEAR PLASTIC AS A FAST-AND-EASY COLDFRAME.

KITCHEN GADGETS IN THE GARDEN

When you're looking around for great garden gadgets, don't forget to check your kitchen! Paring knives are great tools for weeding flower gardens. If there's a weed close to a plant, just slip the knife close to the stem and flick it away from the plant. These narrow-bladed knives are also great for weeding between bricks or in cracks in concrete and asphalt walkways. It's easy to lose these handy little knives among your plants. To avoid wasting time searching for them, dab their handles with a bit of bright paint so you can spot them easily in the garden.

Marianne Kaufman, a volunteer at the Minnesota Landscape Arboretum, has found a new use for another kitchen utensil: She keeps a pair of stainless steel salad tongs in her gardening toolbox. "They're ideal for pulling weeds around rose bushes," explains Kaufman. Like magic, this ordinary kitchen utensil extends your reach while keeping thorns at a safe distance from your hands.

SLIDE IT IN A SAUCER

When her son outgrew his plastic snow-sliding saucer, Sally Roth of New Harmony, Indiana, commandeered it for her garden. "When my clay soil gets wet, it turns into mud that easily sucks in a loaded wheelbarrow so deep that it's hard to budge. But the plastic sled slides right over the top, no matter how heavy I have it piled."

Roth uses the plastic saucer to haul weeds, sticks, compost, manure, transplants, and "just about everything." She notes that it doesn't require much muscle to move the sled around, either, because she can take advantage of body strength rather than arm strength. "I loop the pull rope behind my head across the back of my neck and then under my arms," she describes, "so that it's the chest and shoulders that lean into it, not my already overworked arms or back."

Roth modified the sled by poking a pair of holes near the rim to hold the rope. The plastic handle that came with it was too flimsy to hold up to heavy work.

A LONG-FORGOTTEN CHILD'S SNOW SAUCER IS PERFECT FOR SLIDING LOADS OF GARDEN MATERIALS OVER SLIPPERY CLAY SOIL OR WET GRASS.

NOT JUST FOR CLOTHES

An old-fashioned laundry aid is just the gadget for drying herbs, says Deborah Burdick of Mt. Vernon, Indiana, who grows a selection of culinary flavorings.

"Most of my herbs dry fast, in a week or less," she says, "which is a good thing because my space is limited. I use a wooden fold-out clothes drying rack to hang the herbs. The air circulates well around them, just as it would for clothes, and they're dry in days. I can even use it outside in the shade for herbs that dry really fast, like parsley. And the rack folds flat, which makes it easy to slip in a storage space."

Burdick notes that wooden fold-out clothes drying racks, although well made and durable,

ON HAND: Plastic soda bottle

TURN IT INTO: Flower vase giveaway

HOW TO DO IT: Remove the label from the bottle, using hot water or a sticky substance remover (such as Goo Gone) to get rid of the adhesive, then carefully cut off the top one- to two-thirds of the bottle. Cut some flowers from your garden and take them to a friend!

are surprisingly inexpensive. "You can find them in just about any discount store for about $10," she says.

NIGHT LIGHT

Do you ever find yourself gardening after dark? An organic farmer from Homestead, Florida, Andres Mejides does. He often works all day caring for zoo animals, then heads out to teach a class on organic gardening to local gardeners. It's dark by the time he arrives home, but his crops still need tending, so a good work light is a necessity. "At first, I tried a coal miner's-style headlamp, but too many bugs flew into my face. And, living in tropical Florida, those bugs were *big*." His solution? Portable fluorescent light fixtures fastened to old lamp stands or tripods. Simply attach these battery-operated lights to a stand with wire, clamps, or straps. If your ground is soft enough, you can also just strap a light onto a length of rebar (concrete reinforcing bar) and poke it into the soil where you need to work.

NO-SLIP KNEE PADS

Most gardeners approach knee pads like warriors putting on armor for battle. They pull the straps as tight as possible and vow, "This time, they're going to stay in place." But after just a few deep knee bends and a little crawling through the cannas, knee pads usually wind up halfway down to the ankles.

"Knee pads just don't fasten right. They don't stay in place," fumes Leota Cornett of Roanoke, Virginia. "I looked at my dirty knees one day and said, 'I wish I could attach those knee pads right to my pants.' " And that's exactly what she did. Cornett cut large pieces of fabric out of some old blue jeans and used them to sew a big "pocket" on each knee of another pair of pants. Then she slipped a piece of foam rubber padding into each pocket. "Now my knee pads are always in place," Cornett says. When her gardening pants need to be washed, Cornett just slides the foam pads out of the pockets.

ON HAND: Old carving fork

TURN IT INTO: A soil cultivator

HOW TO DO IT: A stainless-steel carving fork makes a handy tool for scratching fertilizer into garden beds, says Don Engebretson of Minneapolis, Minnesota. He adds that using the fork with a plunge-and-twist motion quickly loosens compacted soil, and it's great for weeding in tight places, too.

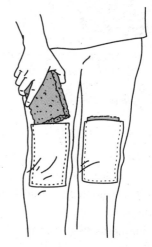

HAVING TROUBLE WITH SLIPPERY KNEE PADS? SEW KNEE PAD "POCKETS" ON THE KNEES OF YOUR GARDEN PANTS.

DRESSED TO TILL

If you spot Barbara Ashmun, the author of *The Garden Design Primer*, you might mistake her for a surgeon, a fisherman, or a welder. That's because she shops for her gardening togs at industrial stores, not gardening boutiques!

First stop is the sporting goods store where she finds her favorite rubber boots and a fishing vest (those small, zippered pockets and pouches are ideal for holding garden tags, notebooks, markers, twine, tissues, and any other small items). When she needs gloves, she visits a local medical supply store to pick up a box of disposable surgical gloves. Ashmun says these are great for keeping hands clean and dry while still allowing your fingers to move freely. These inexpensive gloves only cost about 6 cents a pair, but they'll last for a few hours of weeding or a whole day of potting up before they tear or get too clammy. If heavier chores are in store, Ashmun suggests picking up a well-priced pair of tough gloves at a welding-supply shop.

HELPING HANDLES

After a day of wielding tools in the garden, even strong hands can get tired, but it's especially difficult if you have arthritis. Cheryl Coston of Fairdealing, Missouri, has found a way to ease the pain by softening the handles of hand tools such as rakes, hoes, trowels, and even pruners. All it takes is a package or two of inexpensive foam pipe insulation, available at discount and hardware stores for about $4 for a pack of four or five pieces. She uses the long, large-diameter pieces of this cylindrical insulation to cover longer-handled tools like rakes and hoes. "Just slip it on, press the sticky edges together, and the grip is now larger and cushioned," she says. For hand tools, she cuts the smaller-diameter lengths of insulation to fit and slips them on the same way.

Sometimes Coston takes her handling just a step further. If the insulation is a bit loose on the handle, she wraps red tape a few times around the foam in a spiral. That also makes the

ON HAND: Old ironing board

TURN IT INTO: Portable potting bench

HOW TO DO IT: Simply remove the padded cover and set it up wherever you want to work. Barbara Ashmun, the author of *Garden Retreats*, loves the fact that the surface is smooth, and the whole thing can be folded and stored just about anywhere.

tools easier to spot in the garden and the shed. "The original foam has been on my long-handled tools for years," she says. "Harder-working trowels get new foam every 2 years. This has really helped the arthritis in my hands. I no longer need gloves just to use a tool, and with all the red handles, I rarely lose a tool anymore!"

VERSATILE PLANT FLATS

Plastic mesh plant flats have myriad uses aside from transporting plants. Position them over flats of seedlings that you're taking outside to harden off. Or set flats of plants on top of an upturned mesh flat to provide better air circulation and drainage. In the garden, use flats to cover

Build It!

RUSTIC LOG BENCH

Leave no stone (or in this case—log) unturned! This handmade log bench can double as a side table or coffee table. Native red cedar (*Juniperus virginiana*) and white birch (*Betula pendula*) are great woods for this project, but others would work equally well. Linda Harris, of Fulton, Kentucky, suggests looking for logs with holes, branch stubs, and intact bark because these features make the bench more interesting. Dry your selected log for several months in a covered place before you start the project.

Materials

A large log or tree trunk, about 12 inches across and 36 to 48 inches long

4 smaller logs, about 2 to 3 inches across and 12 to 18 inches long

12 nails (about 3 inches long and ⅛ inch in diameter)

Strong wood glue

Saw, wood-chopping hatchet, or log splitter

Hammer

Wood planer, sander, or rasp (optional)

DIRECTIONS

1. Using a saw, hatchet, or splitter, divide the large log in half lengthwise, keeping the cut fairly smooth and flat (it doesn't have to be perfect). Select one log half for the bench. Leave the bark, the branch stubs, and the saw marks for a rustic look. If you prefer a smoother surface, sand or plane the flat top surface or smooth it with a rasp.

---

young seedlings to protect them from wind, light frost, and nibbling critters. Mesh strawberry baskets make good individual plant cover-ups as well.

LAVENDER INSTEAD OF LAUNDRY

Another clothes-drying apparatus is favored by paper artist Pat Hoskins, who grows herbs and flowers to use in her artwork. "My clothesline is the easiest spot I know to dry herbs and flowers," says Hoskins, who loosely bundles the fresh material with cotton string, then clips the string to her clothesline with spring-type clothespins.

Hoskins keeps a ball of string and a child's pair of scissors in her clothespin bag for easy access when the mood strikes her. "I can clip geranium flowers, yarrow, lavender, whatever I

2. The finished height of the bench equals the leg length plus the thickness of the top log. To make the bench legs, cut the smaller logs to equal lengths. Choose the most attractive side of each smaller log to be the outer-facing side, then mark the opposite side with a pencil.

3. Saw the top and bottom ends of each of the smaller logs at about a 20-degree angle, putting the small angle on the outer side of each leg to create a slanted leg.

4. Turn the large log flat side down. Mark the positions for the four legs (the bench will be sturdier if the legs are close to the log end).

5. Using a helper to hold each log leg in place, place the leg's angled cut against the rounded part of the log and hammer three nails into each leg from different angles, driving the nails through the leg and into the bench.

6. Turn the bench right side up. Plane, sand, or rasp a little wood off the bottoms of the legs to get rid of any wobbling.

7. Turn the bench upside down again and apply glue at each of the four leg joins. Allow the glue to dry thoroughly. Apply clear finish, if you wish, and allow it to dry thoroughly before using.

OUTSIDE OF LEG

NAILS

have blooming, and hang it from the clothesline in just a minute or two, so I have a constant supply of new dried flowers for my projects." She uses the shadier end of the clothesline to dry her plant materials, so the sun doesn't fade blossoms. "They turn out so nice, I've started using them to make little wreaths and dried bouquets for friends and to decorate gift packages, too."

BUCKET SEAT

Gardeners with stiff knees or a long job appreciate a place to sit while working. Pat Hoskins of Evansville, Indiana, found that a plastic 5-gallon bucket makes a perfect perch for tending her raised beds.

"It's strong, sturdy, and stable," she says. "Plus it's easy to pick up and move with me from place to place."

ON HAND: Old Frisbee

TURN IT INTO: Plant saucer, a butterfly bath, and more

HOW TO DO IT: Elsa Efran of Philadelphia finds new ways to use old Frisbees. They work well as temporary plant saucers, as dishes to hold cut melon halves in the refrigerator, as wind- and sunbreaks for new transplants, and as seed soakers. She fills them with water to create an instant bird or butterfly bath. She even pours beer into them and then sets them in her garden to trap marauding slugs.

recycling bin. They do: Just ask Cheryl Coston of Fairdealing, Missouri. In fact, for her, they serve more than one garden purpose. First, she cuts off the top of the container just above the handle to make a sturdy scoop for organic fertilizers or other materials. "I marked measurements on the outside so I could scoop the right amount to shake directly into my beds," she says. With the top cut off, the bottles also become handy garden carryalls. You can use them to tote trowels, other small tools, seeds, and necessities to and from the garden. Or put a little water in the bottom and use it when collecting flowers from the garden. "It's not as pretty as a basket," she says, "but your flowers will last longer when you put them into water right after you cut them."

No Mud in the House

"You could always tell when I'd been out in the garden," says herbalist and gardener Valerie West of St. Phillips, Indiana. "No matter how thoroughly I thought I'd cleaned my shoes on the boot scraper or the doormat, I would drop packed mud from between my shoe treads as I walked around the house. And if I'm just coming in to get a drink or to check my phone messages, I don't want to waste time taking them off and putting them back on. Now I keep a sturdy, flat-tip screwdriver beside the front door. It takes just a minute to pry out the caked mud from the tread of my boots."

Hoskins got her garden seats from a nearby restaurant, where they're free for the asking. She says she often uses two buckets at once: one to sit on and one to carry compost or hold trimmings and weeds.

DETERGENT-BOTTLE CONVERSIONS

It seems as though those heavy-duty plastic, squarish detergent containers should have some use, other than taking up space in the

TOMATO CAGE HOLIDAY TREE

When removing the tomato cages from the garden at the end of the season, save one to use as a holiday centerpiece. To decorate, wrap grapevine around the cage, securing it with wire. Turn the cage upside down, string white lights on it, and plug it in! The cone-shaped "tree" looks beautiful indoors or out. When the New Year arrives, "untrim" the tree—or store it as is. When the holidays roll around again, you can put up the tree in minutes!

From Sweaters to Sundried Tomatoes

If you have a mesh sweater drying rack on hand, you have an instant tomato dryer, too! Deborah Burdick of Mt. Vernon, Indiana, sometimes makes her drying rack do double-duty as a fruit and vegetable dryer in the sun. "When I harvest extra tomatoes, I slice them and spread them on sweater drying screens that I lay across the dowels of a wooden drying rack. In our hot Indiana summers, I can have sundried tomatoes by the end of the day." She drapes an old nylon window curtain over the rack to keep bugs away from the drying food.

ON HAND: An old plastic shower curtain

TURN IT INTO: Leaf catcher and planting tote

HOW TO DO IT: Place flats and small tools on the curtain, and drag it to the spot where you're working, says Linda Harris of Fulton, Kentucky. Or fill it with leaves you need to haul away. (Just make sure to keep your hauls at less than 20 pounds, or else the curtain might tear.)

Pest Control

Garden pests come in all shapes and sizes. And, unfortunately, there is no universal pest control technique. In this chapter, though, we've compiled a plethora of pest-deterrent tips and recipes. Find out how "Foil Collars Deter Cutworms and Slugs" and how to build a "Portable Porcupine Excluder." We've even provided a fantastic recipe for deer repellent.

FOIL COLLARS DETER CUTWORMS AND SLUGS

Foil hungry cutworms with aluminum foil, says gardener Anita Nielsen of Saugatuck, Michigan. Nielson had no luck keeping cutworms and slugs away from tender young cabbage, pepper, and tomato seedlings until she tried making plant collars out of aluminum foil. "It's just so easy. I have *no* cutworm problem at all," Nielsen says. To make a collar, she cuts a piece of aluminum foil about 6 inches square and then crumples it slightly. "Just until it feels rough to the touch," she explains. Then Nielsen tears the foil from the middle of one side to the center of the square. She slips the plant stem through that opening and pinches the foil closed around the stem, forming something like a mini-tree guard. "You just have to be sure that the foil covers the stem and reaches down into the soil just a little bit," Neilsen cautions.

SLUG DISCOURAGEMENT

Discourage slugs in the garden by sprinkling red cedar shavings (the kind used for hamster litter) around your plants. According to Carole Carpenter Russell, teacher and gardener, of Union City, Tennessee, "They hate crawling over the cedar."

SLUGS SAY OUCH

"I've found a successful and inexpensive way to discourage slugs," says Caroline Whitenack of Doylestown, Pennsylvania. "I take a bucket of builder's sand to the garden with me when I'm transplanting. When I set each plant in the ground, I use an old laundry scoop to distribute sand around the base of each small plant. Slugs won't crawl over the sharp sand."

CUP O' DEER REPELLENT

After having too many antlered visitors at his orchard, Jerald Deal of Deal's Orchard in Jefferson, Iowa, concocted this deterrent made from simple materials.

He asked his local barber to save him a bag or two of human hair. Then he wrapped a fistful of human hair into a square of nylon netting and tied it into a bundle with a string.

To protect the hair from rain—which can wash away the human smell and make the deterrent ineffective—he poked a hole in the bottom of a 12-ounce plastic foam cup. He placed the bundle in the cup, pulled the string through the hole, and tied it into a loop.

Deal hangs one cup per tree and replaces the cup each year. He says this tricks deer for about 3 years before they catch on and he has to find another clever way of keeping them out of his orchard.

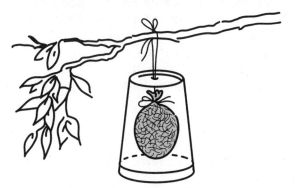

THE DEER-REPELLING SCENT OF HUMAN HAIR LASTS LONGER WHEN SHELTERED FROM WEATHER BY A CUP.

CATCH MORE FLIES WITH HONEY

When Cleveland garden writer Thea Steinmetz found flies and gnats buzzing around her greenhouse, she remembered watching her mother make homemade honey flypaper back in Germany. Thea's adaptation of her mom's technique starts with cutting smallish pieces of yellow construction paper and smearing them with warmed honey. She then props them up in the greenhouse beds with a recycled card holder from a florist shop or simply in the tines of an old kitchen fork. The flying nasties are at-

ON HAND: Empty 5½-ounce cat food cans

TURN THEM INTO: Cutworm collars

HOW TO DO IT: Wash the cans thoroughly, cut the bottoms off, and remove the labels. Place them over transplants and press them into the ground to prevent cutworms from chewing off tender plants.

tracted to the color and the sweetness, only to become stuck in the honey. When the sticky paper is coated with bugs, she simply discards it and makes a new piece.

APPLE TRAP ANYONE?

Don't let your next wild tennis serve end up in George Weigel's yard: He may paint it red and hang it from his apple tree! No, this garden writer for the Harrisburg, Pennsylvania, *Patriot-News* hasn't gone mad—he has just found an inexpensive solution to apple pests. Weigel takes old tennis balls, spray paints them bright red, and then sticks a stiff piece of coat hanger wire through each one. He bends one end of the wire into a simple hook and curves the other end up so the ball won't

Build It!

A POP-APART ROW-COVER FRAME

"I'd rather spend 15 minutes installing a row cover than waste hours chasing after flighty cucumber beetles day after day," says Alabama gardener Barbara Pleasant. "Plus, row covers frustrate rabbits hungry for a taste of lettuce and keep deer from rummaging after my bush beans."

Row covers work best when they rest on a frame over the plants so that the fabric can't rub against tender new leaves. Pleasant came up with this pop-apart row-cover frame to do the job. "I saw some other gardeners using PVC pipe arches to hold bird netting over their berries, so I adapted their method to make this row-cover frame," she says. "It works beautifully when placed over wide rows. And when I'm not using it, the whole thing pops apart for easy storage against a wall of the garage. But it doesn't stay in storage long because it's always in use!"

Materials

Six 3-foot lengths of
½-inch-diameter PVC pipe

Two ½-inch PVC T-connectors

Two 24-inch pieces of
½-inch-diameter PVC pipe

½-inch PVC cross connector

10 × 10-foot piece of
Reemay or other floating
row cover

Hand saw or utility knife

Sawhorse

---

slip off. He then wraps each one with a sandwich bag (secured by a rubber band at the top) and coats each bag with Tangle-Trap (a sticky material available at garden centers) or even petroleum jelly. By hanging three or four of the gooey look-alike apples in each tree before the real fruit turns red, he attracts and traps apple pests and limits their damage to his apples.

FLY SUCKER

Whiteflies getting in your face? Try busting them away with your battery-operated vacuum cleaner, suggests Thea Steinmetz, a scented-geranium lover in Cleveland, Ohio. Whiteflies love geraniums, she explains, so when they get to be a bother, she simply shakes the stem of each plant with one hand to stir up the flies and sucks them up with her handheld vacuum

DIRECTIONS

1. Cut PVC pipe into pieces with a hand saw or utility knife. Use a sawhorse to support the pipe as you cut it.

2. Fit two 3-foot pieces into one of the T-connectors to form a section of pipe that's about 6 feet long. Do the same with two more 3-foot pieces and the second connector. (These sections will form the ends of the frame). Fit the remaining 3-foot pieces into the cross con-nector to form the middle support of the frame.

3. Gently bend one end piece into a semicircle and push the ends 10 inches or more into the ground on either side of the row or bed, about 6 inches from where you want the end of the tunnel to be. Place one of the 24-inch long pieces into the T-connector at the top of the frame.

4. Bend the middle piece of the frame into an arch, and push the ends into the ground about 24 inches from the end piece so that the free end of the 24-inch piece of pipe fits firmly into the cross-connector.

5. Place the remaining 24-inch piece of pipe into the other side of the cross-connector. Bend the remaining long piece of pipe and push the ends into the ground 24 inches from the middle arch. Pop the end of the 24-inch piece of pipe into the T-connector.

6. Cover the frame with row cover, and secure the edges with boards or bricks. When you disassemble the frame to move or store it, the arched pieces of pipe will retain their shape.

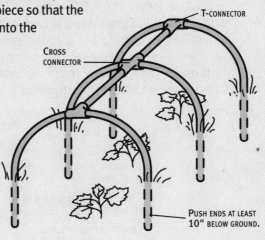

T-CONNECTOR

CROSS CONNECTOR

PUSH ENDS AT LEAST 10" BELOW GROUND.

---

cleaner. Within 3 or 4 days, the fly population plummets and the plants go outside for a good hosing down. The result? No more whiteflies!

VINEGAR DUNK STILLS THE JAPANESE BEETLE BRIGADE

Japanese beetles can be a real menace to roses, corn, raspberries, and many ornamentals. For short-term control, hand-picking is the safest and most effective measure. To make the job easier, place cans of vinegar solution (equal parts apple cider vinegar and water) next to vulnerable plants. Early and late in the day when beetles are sluggish, hold the can under the beetles and knock them into the vinegar solution. Vinegar kills them quickly but isn't harmful to kids or pets. Leave the can in place until it's full, and then empty dead bugs into

(continued on page 61)

Build It!

PORTABLE PORCUPINE EXCLUDER

For 20 years Mary Zahn's raspberry patch in Juneau, Alaska, was a salad bar for the neighborhood porcupines. "Finally," she says, "I decided I had to be smart enough to outwit these guys, so I designed a cage"—for the berries, that is. Zahn's clever cage is made of screen-wire panels that hook together; you remove them one at a time to pick the berries. (Don't let the canes grow through the wire or you won't be able to get the panels off!) Zahn puts up the cage the minute she spies the first buds in spring—"Porkies love the first new leaves," she says, "Don't procrastinate or you'll lose everything." Throughout the growing season the greenery conceals the wire; in the fall, Zahn takes the cage apart and stashes it in the garage. The number of panels you need to build depends on the size of your raspberry patch—and on your own size and strength. You want the panels small enough that you can comfortably lift them off and reach across to pick the berries. You could also use this cage to protect blueberries, tomatoes, and other crops and to help keep out rabbits and woodchucks.

Materials

Four 12-inch lengths of PVC piping, about 4¼ inches in diameter

Four 2 × 4s, the height of your mature plants plus 12 inches

Wood scraps or rocks

Twenty 2 × 2s of a height and width to make frames that you can handle comfortably

Wood screws or nails, as needed

Chicken wire

1 × 2s, short sections, as needed

16 sets of hooks and eyes

Four 10-inch bungie cords

Staple gun and staples

Screwdriver

DIRECTIONS

1. Measure out the area you want for your raspberry patch, and sink one length of PVC piping 12 inches into the ground at each corner of your plot.

2. Insert a 2 × 4 into each pipe, wedging it with scrap wood or rocks if necessary to hold it steady.

3. Build the frames for the side panels and the top panel using the 2 × 2s and nails. Cut sections of chicken wire large enough to cover each frame, and staple the chicken wire in place. To strengthen the cage, screw short sections of 1 × 2s for corner brackets to the frame.

4. Screw a hook into the outside corner of each chicken-wire panel so that the hook points downward.

5. Screw two eyes at the top and bottom of each 2 × 4 (on adjacent corners as shown below), measuring to make sure the eyes will line up with the hooks you've placed on the panels so the panels will hang straight.

6. Fit the side panels into place.

7. If birds or deer are a problem, fasten a top panel onto the frame with the bungie cords. Loop a cord through the chicken wire at each corner and fasten the hooks to the frame or the wire on the side panels.

8. Use rocks to fill any gaps between frame and ground.

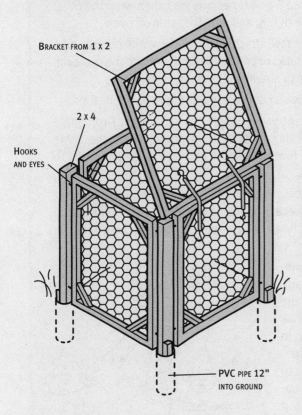

BRACKET FROM 1 X 2

2 X 4

HOOKS AND EYES

PVC PIPE 12" INTO GROUND

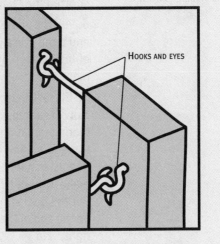

HOOKS AND EYES

Build It!

Fun Scarecrow

"I like my scarecrows to look good. If they also help scare the crows away, that's good too," says Linda Harris of Fulton, Kentucky. "The head I've used here helps make some noise. Move the scarecrow around the garden to keep the birds guessing and the neighbors amused."

Materials

One 3- to 4-foot 1 × 2, for arms

One 6- to 8-foot 1 × 2, for upright

Heavy twine

Old shirt, pants, or skirt and shirt

Tacks or brads

Galvanized 1-gallon bucket

Waterproof paint or permanent markers (optional)

Old pantyhose

10 to 12 metal jingle bells

Twine, ribbon, or a scarf

Directions

1. Position the shorter piece of lumber perpendicular to and about 12 inches below one end of the longer piece.

2. Lash pieces together by wrapping twine around the join, making an X. Wrap 3 or 4 times one way, then wrap the other way, pulling twine tightly, and repeat. Fasten off twine.

3. Dress the scarecrow, attaching the clothing with only the minimum number of tacks or brads along the arms, so the fabric can float free and flap or stream in the wind.

4. Turn bucket upside down and paint a face on it, if desired.

5. Put one pantyhose leg inside the other one. Drop jingle bells inside stocking foot, tie knot about where the ankle would be. Add a few more knots between ankle and waist to shorten the "hat."

6. Pull the waist of the pantyhose down over bottom of bucket and tightly tie a piece of twine, ribbon, or a scarf around the lip of bucket (top of head but bottom of bucket) to keep "hat" in place.

7. Place the scarecrow in garden, hammering down on the top end to sink it as deeply as needed to make it stand firm. Put the bucket head on the end of the upright, and give your creation a name!

PANTYHOSE

FACE MADE WITH WATERPROOF PAINT

the compost pile and refill the cans. This is a great job for youngsters eager to earn vacation money! Over time, hand-picking can reduce beetle problems significantly.

BOARDS FOIL BIRDS

"Grackles and other blackbirds love to snatch up my pea seeds as soon as I plant them," says gardener and author Sally Roth of New Harmony, Indiana. "I like the blackbirds, but I also wanted peas. So I turned to an old trick my mother used in her big family garden when I was a child. After I plant and water the rows, I lay 2 × 4s or any other scrap boards I have around over the peas. I lift the boards after a few days to check whether the seeds are sprouting. When I see they've broken ground, I take off the boards. The seedlings green up in just a day or two. Once the peas sprout, the birds aren't as interested in them."

Sally says hiding peas under a board has another advantage: "The board keeps the soil nice and moist around the seeds, so my crop sprouts days faster than uncovered rows. And I don't have to water in the meantime."

RED-HOT SQUIRRELS

Did you know that you could use an old spice jar with a perforated lid to sprinkle cayenne pepper around your young transplants to repel squirrels? It not only works to keep

ON HAND: Clear plastic 12- to 16-ounce water or soda bottles

TURN THEM INTO: Cutworm barriers

HOW TO DO IT: Slice plastic bottles into 3-inch-high rings, then press into soil about 1 inch over newly planted seedlings. They make a very effective cutworm barrier, according to Irv Breber of Bensalem, Pennsylvania, and they don't show from a distance.

squirrels out of your beds, but it also keeps squirrels off the bird feeder. And best of all, the cayenne pepper doesn't seem to bother the birds.

Planters

Believe it or not, just about anything can be a planter. In this section, find out how you can use gourds, drawers, bushel baskets, buckets, plastic-foam coolers, tires, or plungers as containers for both outdoor and indoor plantings.

GOURD PLANTERS

Birdhouse gourds are good for more than just birdhouses. These gracefully shaped gourds also make beautifully shaped planters for all types of annuals, herbs, and even strawberries.

To grow a self-supporting gourd pot, position developing gourds on pieces of wood in your garden so the bottoms become flat. When the gourds have matured, harvest, dry thoroughly, and scrape off the flaky skin. Cut off the top of each gourd and drill a few holes in the bottom for drainage. Decorate with paint (if you feel creative) or shellac to help preserve them. If you have a gourd without a flat base, prepare it as above but drill three extra holes in the rim; add rope to enjoy it as a hanging basket.

SOUVENIR MULCH

Rob Cardillo and his wife, Sue, of Ambler, Pennsylvania, love houseplants, but their dog Stella loves them even more! Too many times, they found her munching away at the potting soil of the bigger plants that sat on the floor. Unable to persuade Stella to eat a more sensible diet, they resolved to put a stone mulch over the potting soil to discourage her late-night raids.

As they began to look for suitable pebbles, they realized they already had dozens of beautiful stones and shells brought home as souvenirs from their many travels throughout the world. By artfully placing them around each plant, they not only solved the dog problem, they also found the perfect way to display their exotic rocks. "Plus," Sue adds, "they glisten and shine every time we water."

GARDENS-TO-GO

Bushel baskets make ideal container gardens and the price is right. "I buy used baskets from the crab house for $2 a piece. A good hosing takes care of the fishy smell," says Tina James, a resourceful Maryland gardener, with a laugh. James lines the baskets with plastic bags, being sure to slash a few holes for drainage, and fills them with potting soil. She also adds a shovelful of compost to these basket containers. "Compost inoculates that sterilized potting soil with the microorganisms that support soil life, which in turns supports plant growth." Besides being cheap, James says the baskets are large enough to accommodate a mini salad-and-herb garden. "I plant lettuce, radishes, parsley, violas, and onion sets in the spring and then replant for the summer with bush beans, basil, and calendulas. If you position the basket near a railing or outfit it with a trellis, you can add vines like morning glories or cucumbers."

As a bonus, the baskets are portable—they even have handles! James likes to present them as gifts to shut-in gardening friends. "I've carried the baskets filled with dry potting soil up to the 11th floor of an apartment building with no trouble. Add the plants and water after the basket reaches its destination.

For best results, put something under the basket so it's not in direct contact with the ground or the deck—bricks, slates, or wood blocks work fine. The basket drains better and the increased air circulation retards rot." James says her gardens-to-go last for two seasons. Not bad for $2.

Bubble Window Greenhouses

A plastic bubble window well protector makes a simple and inexpensive greenhouse—and you can pick one up at a home-supply store for less than $5. To use, place the bubble window against the wall of a shed or garage. Simply lift it up to move tender plants and seedlings in and out. Remember—you have to vent the bubble window just as you would any cold-frame or greenhouse, or the space will quickly overheat when the sun is out. In early spring, use a brick to prop the window ajar a few inches. Once the weather is warmer, stand the

ON HAND: An old drawer from a kitchen or bathroom remodeling project or from old furniture

TURN IT INTO: A portable raised bed

HOW TO DO IT: Just drill several holes in the bottom of the drawer for drainage, fill with soil, and plant.

brick on one end to hold the window higher off the ground. Eventually, you can remove the window during the day and replace it in the late afternoon to shelter plants from nighttime chills. If temperatures threaten to plummet below freezing, drape a wool blanket over the bubble for added protection because plastic retains only a few degrees of extra heat once the sun goes down.

Plumber's and Florist's Helper

A plumber's helper can be a creative part of a topiary arrangement, says Philadelphia florist Bill Franklin, who often gives demonstrations at the Philadelphia Flower Show. Franklin paints a plumber's helper (or plunger) green, and sticks it handle-end down into floral foam in an

ON HAND: New or used coffee filters

TURN THEM INTO: Large pot liners

HOW TO DO IT: Place coffee filters in the bottoms of larger pots before adding growing medium to keep soil from sifting out. Andrea Ray Chandler, a Master Gardener who hails from Olathe, Kansas, also suggests using shredded pieces of old spun-polyester row covers or old pantyhose in this manner.

arranging container. He then does matching arrangements in the plunger cup and in the container, making it look like a plant that has been grown as a standard.

DESIGNER CONTAINERS FOR A FRACTION OF THE PRICE

Container gardening is all the rage, but buying lots of interesting-looking containers can get expensive. Linda Harris of Fulton,

Kentucky, shares her clever idea for making her own—at a much lower cost than retail! Harris uses the bowl of an old round charcoal grill for casting containers. She mixes and pours concrete into the bowl, spreads it out to edges, and shapes the inner surface of the bowl as desired. "Shallow containers cast like this make nice planters for sedums, cacti, and ground covers.

"For decorative containers, I like to put pebbles or shells in first, like you put the pineapple in first for an upside-down cake, then pour the concrete," says Harris. She adds that this type of container makes an equally nice birdbath. In that case, you might want to press pebbles, shells or pieces of colored glass into the inside surface for a designer look.

POTATOES ABOVE THE GROUND

Another way to use a stacked bin composter for growing crops is to turn it into an above-ground potatoes planter. Simply unstack the sections in an open, sunny area with good drainage. Fill the first section with compost mixed with garden soil, and plant your potato tubers just deep enough to cover the tuber. As the plants grows, add the second and third sections of the composter. (Fill them with the compost/soil mixture, too.) When it's harvest time, says Susan LeMaster, who grows her spuds in Portland, Oregon, take the sections apart and the taters fall out—no muss, no fuss, no digging.

EASY RAISED HERB BED

Those "tire gardens" many people make fun of still work very well, especially for herbs which tend to spread out and sprawl over the edge of the tire. Use a big old tire from a car, truck, or tractor. "What's especially nice about gardening in a raised bed like this is you get both moisture retention and excellent drainage, which is preferred by herbs such as lavender, oregano, sage, and thyme," advises Linda Harris of Fulton, Kentucky. "And kids get a kick out of gardening in a tire, which could help them develop a lifetime hobby of gardening."

Harris says you can set the tire down in an existing garden or on lawn grass; you don't need to dig the sod layer up. Then fill the tire with a mixture of garden soil and packaged soilless potting mixture. "This raised area in the garden works nicely to accent the plants, such as purple basil or variegated thyme. And plants around the tire can cover it up if you don't like its looks."

CHILLY CHEST PLANTER

Sometimes a gardener has too many plants for one place or one planting effort. One way to heel them in (keep plants for a short time before you actually get them planted) is to pot up in temporary containers the way Lois Stringer of Bellefonte, Pennsylvania, does. "I've found that plastic-foam ice chests do the trick for up to about 2 weeks. The chests also make inexpensive patio planters for colorful summer plantings. They really hold the soil moisture well, which is great in dry climates."

TRAYS OF LIGHT

Wash out and save those throwaway aluminum baking pans; they make excellent water trays for plants and seedlings because the aluminum reflects light back on to the plants.

ON HAND: An old stacked-bin composter

TURN IT INTO: Mini-raised beds

HOW TO DO IT: First, loosen the ground where you want the beds to go. Unstack the sections, fill them with a mix of half compost and half soil, and plant. Says Master Gardener Judy Wong of Menlo Park, California, "I use the sections for lettuce, which likes good drainage and good air circulation."

Using aluminum trays can result in a noticeable growth spurt in plants. They're especially good for houseplants in a shady place.

CREATIVE CONTAINERS

Want to give your plants interesting homes without spending a lot of money on containers? Then make your own using recycled items from around your house the way Linda Harris of Fulton, Kentucky, does. Sometimes an unusual container can bring a smile, so use your imagi-

Build It!

MINI PLANT NURSERY AND TOOL SHED

A nursery bed is a handy place to grow seedlings until they are ready for the garden, but what if all your space is already filled with plants? George Weigel, garden writer for the Harrisburg, Pennsylvania, *Patriot-News,* designed and built this waist-high seedling bed out of scrap lumber. He uses it as an outdoor nursery for vegetable seedlings to replace plants that he yanks out of the garden during the growing season. Because it's on legs, you don't have to bend over to use it—a bonus for gardeners with bad backs or trick knees. "The real kicker is that I mounted an old mailbox on the bottom to store my row markers, pruners, string, trowel, and all those other little things that I always used to forget back in the garage."

Materials

Four 24-inch 2 × 6s	Four 36-inch 2 × 4s
3-inch galvanized nails or screws	Two 27-inch 2 × 4s
Two 24 × 27-inch pieces of ½- or ¾-inch plywood	Primer and paint, or polyurethane
¼-inch galvanized nails or screws	Hammer or screwdriver
	Drill with ⅜-inch bit

DIRECTIONS

1. Fasten together the 2 × 6s to form the seedling box, using 3-inch nails or screws.

2. Fasten one piece of plywood to the bottom of the assembled box with 1¼-inch nails or screws. Drill ⅜-inch drainage holes spaced 6 inches apart in the plywood.

nation before you throw something away—it might make an interesting planter. Choose plants that are in scale to the container. If there's no drainage, add a layer of gravel in the bottom before planting. Here are a few ideas: Hens and chicks look great in a beat-up boot or old running shoe. Try herbs in your old saucepan with a ripped-up nonstick coating. A chipped soup tureen is another fine container for herbs. A fern in a fishbowl or geraniums in a bucket are two more fun and fitting ideas.

CINDER BLOCKS FOR SEDUM

Cinder blocks (the ones with holes that go all the way through) make nice containers for sedums and succulents. "I think of cinder blocks

3. Attach the 36-inch 2 × 4 legs to the outer sides of the box with 3-inch nails or screws.

4. Fasten the 27-inch 2 × 4 leg supports to the legs, a couple of inches up from the bottom of the legs, with 3-inch nails or screws.

5. Attach the plywood shelf to the supports with 1¼-inch nails or screws.

6. Add a coat of paint (prime the wood first!) or polyurethane over the entire piece to help protect it from the elements.

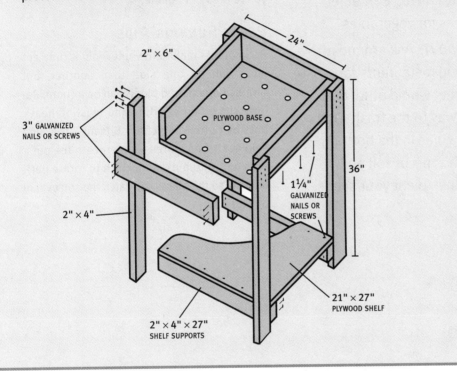

as the economy-conscious strawberry jar," says Linda Harris of Fulton, Kentucky. Set a block on its side so the holes are on top and fill the holes with a mixture of garden soil and packaged soilless potting mixture. Blocks can also be stacked in various ways and then planted with hens and chicks or low-growing sedums. In a very short time, the plants will cover the block.

"Set one of these near the front door for an attractive accent and conversation piece. It's fun to watch the plants grow and bloom."

Plant Taxi

Moving container plants can be a chore, especially when you have a lot of them to move, or you have containers that are heavy. But

ON HAND: Used 5-gallon pickle or mayonnaise buckets

TURN THEM INTO: Container gardens for vegetables

HOW TO DO IT: Ask around at fast-food restaurants for buckets that would otherwise find their way to the trash. Drill drainage holes in the bottom, fill with a mix of soil and compost, then plant your seeds.

with a plant taxi, moving containers is a breeze. All you need is a wooden packing-crate lid, four casters, and four screws. Just screw a caster to each corner of the lid's base—and, presto, easy transit for container plants. To make moving even easier, screw a large eye hook into the middle of one edge of the lid. When it's travel time, snap a rope—or your dog's leash—onto the eye hook and you're ready to ramble.

PLANT SUNNING AIDS

Patio plants make grow unevenly if they get more sun on one side than another, but turning large potted plants can be a chore. Relieve the strain of lifting and twisting heavy pots by putting large lazy Susans—the type sold in kitchen stores—underneath the pots. Pots on turntables are a cinch to rotate periodically so the plants can catch the sun evenly on all sides.

Planting Helpers

One of the joys of being a gardener is at planting time. With every drop of a seed, the promise of a bountiful harvest later in the season hovers in the air. But planting is not always easy. In the following section, you'll read about how you can make this critical, early-season duty less of a chore— and more joyful.

PERFECT MESCLUN PLANTING FRAMES

"My problems with mesclun and baby lettuce were caused partly by spring fever and partly by foraging cutworms," says Alabama gardener Barbara Pleasant. "I tended to plant way too much at one time instead of sowing a few pinches of seed at a time." To solve her problem, Pleasant came up with special planting frames that double as cutworm barriers.

Pleasant makes the frames by using a utility knife to cut the bottom 2 inches off of inexpensive plastic washbasins. "I stick the bottomless frame in the ground with the upper lip about 1 inch above the surface and the sides 2 inches deep in the soil," she explains. With the basin frame as the boundary, scatter seed over the soil inside. This produces a perfect small planting of lettuce, and you'll find that wandering cutworms rarely figure out how to worm their way under the plastic barriers. For a continuous supply of greens, every 2 to 3 weeks, fashion another frame and plant inside it.

CUTWORMS CAN'T MOW DOWN MESCLUN OR BABY LETTUCE PLANTED IN THE PROTECTIVE FRAME OF A BOTTOMLESS PLASTIC WASHBASIN THAT'S PUSHED FIRMLY INTO THE SOIL.

PENNY-PINCHING PLANTER

Do you like to plant a few new bulbs in your garden each year? Leota Cornett of Roanoke, Virginia, does, and she has devised a simple way to keep track of the spots where she wants to add those new bulbs. Each spring, Cornett al-

ON HAND: 15-inch-long metal pipe, at least 1 inch in diameter

TURN IT INTO: Bulb planter

HOW TO DO IT: Pound the pipe into wet ground, pull it out, and drop a small bulb in the hole. Use a stick or dowel to poke out the plug of soil stuck in the pipe, and crumble it over the bulb.

ways notices a few spots where more bulbs would look good. To help her locate those bare spots in fall when it's time to plant, she uses the plastic caps from spray cans, or even empty tuna cans, as planting markers. "You just tramp the caps down in the grass where you want the new bulbs," Cornett explains. "In fall, you scratch around that area until you find the cap. That's exactly where to plant the bulb. I even have a color-coding system," Cornett adds. "If I need to fill in with a blue hyacinth, I find a blue cap to mark the spot."

HOMEMADE SPACING STRIPS

A yardstick can be a great planting aid when you're setting out transplants in the garden, at least until you accidentally kneel on it and— "crack!"—snap it in half. Frustrated by a

growing pile of broken yardsticks, George DeVault, who gardens near Emmaus, Pennsylvania, found the solution in a stack of scrap lumber in his basement.

DeVault found that furring strips—1 × 3-inch boards used to mount wall paneling and ceiling tile—are much sturdier than most yardsticks. To turn furring strips into spacing guides, saw them to length to fit along your garden beds. Then, using a permanent marker, draw lines across both sides of each strip at the desired spacing. DeVault has one customized furring strip each for 8-, 10-, 12-, and 18-inch spacings.

"When I use the guides in a bed with a straight border, it's easy to keep the rows parallel simply by measuring the distance between rows with a shorter piece of furring strip," DeVault explains. The furring strips are thick enough that you can lean or even step lightly on them when working in wide beds. So far, DeVault's homemade spacing strips have lasted 5 years without mishap.

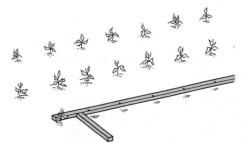

FURRING STRIPS ARE MUCH MORE DURABLE THAN YARDSTICKS AS PLANT SPACING GUIDES.

COFFEE CAN TO THE RESCUE

Tamping the soil firmly around the roots is an important step in planting new trees and shrubs, but it can be an awkward job. You can save yourself some strain by putting together a homemade soil tamper from an empty coffee can, concrete, and a sturdy shovel handle. Drive some nails through the bottom of the handle, as shown in the illustration, and set that end in the can. Mix up the concrete and pour it into the can until it's nearly full. Prop the handle upright until the concrete sets. This tamper is heavy and has a flat bottom, so it's the perfect tool for compressing soil in a planting hole to get rid of air pockets.

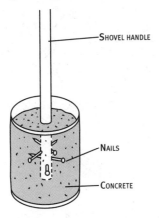

YOU CAN EASILY MAKE THIS SOIL TAMPER WITH JUST A COFFEE CAN, CONCRETE, NAILS, AND A SHOVEL HANDLE.

POST-HOLE DIGGERS: NOT JUST FOR FENCES

Do you own a post-hole digger? If you're planning to install a large planting of perennials or shrubs, you should! Instead of a shovel, use this traditional fencing tool in a new way: to make planting holes for gallon-sized potted plants. It's especially good for planting in tight quarters where you don't have a lot of room to pile the soil next to the hole. To make using this tool less of a "knuckle-buster" when you squeeze the handles together, slip some foam pipe insulation around the handles and secure it with some electrical tape.

NO-BEND PLANTING

Pat Porter of Big River, Saskatchewan, hates bending over when she plants. So she simply cuts a length of slender pipe (metal or smooth PVC would do) about 4 feet long. "Then I just drop the seeds through the pipe and down they go into their place in the ground," Porter says.

This method works better for larger seeds than small ones, but you can use small seeds as long as you mix them with an extender, such as fine, dry sand.

Pennsylvania market gardener Cass Peterson also plants seeds standing up, using a homemade seeder fashioned from a 1-gallon plastic milk jug and a 3-foot piece of plastic pipe. "A 2-liter soda pop bottle will work, too," Peterson says. "Just cut the bottom out of whatever container you're going to use. Solidly attach the plastic pipe to the spout with glue, a hose clamp, or duct tape—whichever works best. Then, just walk down the row, plunking little seeds into the hopper and watching them drop into the furrow—without ever bending over."

SOW SEEDS WITHOUT A LOT OF BACK-BREAKING WORK WITH THE HELP OF A HANDY PIPE PLANTER.

STAND-UP SOWING

Don't throw out that broken umbrella! You can turn it into a great planting gadget! Direct-sowing seed in his quarter-acre garden always left Robert Southam of Nazareth, Pennsylvania, with a pain in the back. The constant bending and stooping made him sore, but if he tried dropping the seeds from a full upright position, they scattered and didn't land where he wanted them to. One day, when Southam was throwing out the trash, he spotted something that would make his task easier: the aluminum stem of a broken umbrella. At about 3 feet long, the light-weight, hollow tube was just what he needed.

Now Southam uses his found seed-sower to plant beans, peas, corn, and most other seed. After making a furrow of the proper depth with a hoe, he puts the seeds he wants to sow in a carpenter's apron he's wearing, and then walks along the furrow with his umbrella handle. As he walks, he places the bottom end in the furrow, and drops the seed through the top, one by one. There's no bending, and every seed falls in its proper place!

CAN'T BEAT IT WITH A STICK

Direct seeding doesn't have to take all day, at least not if you have a custom-made planting stick. Marianne Binetti, a garden columnist from Enumclaw, Washington, says you can make a simple version from just about any piece of long, slender lumber, such as a length of stop-gap molding or a 1 × 2. Make notches or use a permanent marker to mark off every inch the entire length of the lumber. Now you'll have an extra-long yardstick to measure distance between seed plantings.

For a more elaborate version of the planting stick, cut notches into the lumber to create a form that looks like a giant comb. Simply press the planting stick notch-side down into the soil and you'll have a series of perfectly spaced planting holes for seedlings or seeds.

GET PERFECT SPACING EVERY TIME WITH THIS CUSTOM-MADE PLANTING STICK.

EASY PLANTING LINE AND ANCHOR

Using a long string and two stakes to mark straight rows when you plant seeds works just fine—until the string becomes hopelessly tangled. That's why market gardener George DeVault of Emmaus, Pennsylvania, now uses a 100-foot plastic tape measure as a trouble-free planting line. "The tape is bright yellow. It doesn't get dirty and blend with the soil. And when I'm done planting, it takes only a minute to wind it up," DeVault says.

DeVault suggests making special anchors for the tape by sawing a 36-inch, $\frac{1}{4}$-inch-diameter metal rod in half with a hacksaw.

Bend the top 4 inches of each piece of rod to form a handle. It's easy to push these anchors into the ground by hand. Insert one anchor into your garden bed, and put the metal grip at the beginning of the tape over the handle of the anchor. Stretch out the tape, insert the other anchor through the handle of the measuring tape's carrying case, and push it into the soil to keep the tape taut and straight while you work.

HOMEMADE DIBBLE

Sometimes it's the simplest tools that give the best results. Every summer, Frank Conte's tiny front yard garden in Ambler, Pennsylvania, grows sky high with pole beans and tomatoes on an elaborate trellising system that often hides him completely from passersby. And although this 84-year-old Italian immigrant swears that this year's garden will be his last, you'll likely find him next spring planting his beans with a handmade dibble known in the old country as a *pizzucu*. Carved from a piece of bent tree limb, this useful tool fits his hand just as well as his old leather gloves.

To make your own pizzucu, first find a section of bent wood with an angle and girth that fit your hand nicely. Then with your favorite whittling knife, sharpen one end. If you want to get fancy, you can drill a hole in the handle end and loop some rope through so you can hang it up for storage.

HEAVY-DUTY BULB PLANTING

We asked Judy Glattstein "What's the best way to plant flowering bulbs?" and her answer was unequivocal: "With an 8-pound

ON HAND: Old rolling pin

TURN IT INTO: A dibble for making planting holes

HOW TO DO IT: Turn your old wooden pastry roller into a dibble for setting out vegetable and flower transplants. Just turn the roller on its end and press it into the soil to make a perfect planting hole.

mattock!" She should know. This author of *Flowering Bulbs for Dummies* and instructor of a bulb course for professionals at the New York Botanical Gardens has planted more than 22,000 bulbs in the last 4 years at her 9-acre, New Jersey home.

Glattstein knew that planting bulbs with auger drill bits and those tin can-shaped bulb planters would be difficult given her tough rocky-clay soil. Her solution was to loosen entire patches of ground with the mattock, add compost and other soil amendments, and churn everything together. It's easy to plant bulbs in the prepared soil with nothing more than your favorite hand trowel!

Build It!

DIBBLER FRAME FOR MASS PLANTINGS

Need to get lots of small plants into the ground quickly? Follow the lead of Ray McNeilan, a Master Gardener and retired extension agent for Multnomah County, Oregon. He devised this planting tool called a dibbler or dibble when he was propagating azaleas and wanted to get lots of small plants into the ground quickly. It works just as well for groundcover plants or any time you're setting out lots of seedlings.

Adjust the sizes of the 2 × 4s and the number of dibblers to suit your height, the size of your planting area, and the depth and spacing your plants require.

Materials

Galvanized wood screws

Four 3-foot 2 × 4s

Four L-shaped corner braces

1½-inch-diameter wooden dowel, 18 inches long

Screwdriver

Handsaw

DIRECTIONS

1. Screw the 2 × 4s together to make a frame.

2. Screw the four corner braces into place for added support.

3. Saw the dowel into four or six 3-inch pieces, depending on how far apart you want your dibbles spaced.

4. Cut the end of each piece of dowel into a point.

A BULB HAMMER

The idea of a flowering lawn appealed to Rob Cardillo, a garden writer and photographer from Ambler, Pennsylvania. "Wouldn't the front yard look great with scores of early-blooming crocuses and snowdrops pushing up through the grass beneath the old maple trees?" he mused. That fall, he ordered the bulbs and began to plant them under the trees using a standard garden trowel to stab

the ground, pull back the earth, and drop in the bulb. He found out quickly that even with a pointed trowel his hand and arm were cramping as a result of having to stab the ground forcefully to penetrate the root-filled soil. "I knew there had to be a better tool for this job, and I found it in my basement: a standard brick hammer." Used for breaking and setting bricks, this special hammer has a typical hammer face on one side and a long

5. Use screws to attach the dowel pieces to one side of the frame at 8-inch intervals. To do this, predrill holes at 8-inch intervals, then screw each dowel in place.

To use the dibbler, till or spade your garden area. Then mark a series of holes along one outside edge, pressing downward on the dibble to evenly mark off the rows. Then, starting at hole number one, match the outside dibble with the first hole. Hold the dibbler so the individual dibbles will mark a row of planting holes that are perpendicular to the first row you marked. Repeat to mark planting holes across each row, then place transplants in the holes.

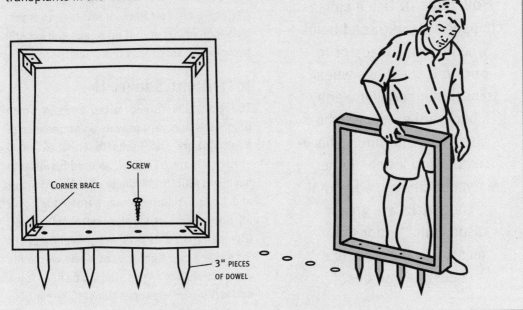

CORNER BRACE

SCREW

3" PIECES OF DOWEL

tapering chisel on the other. The chisel side was perfect for piercing the ground, and the weight and grip of the hammer helped immensely as Cardillo methodically planted his bunches of bulbs.

BETTER BULB PLANTER

She may not be the first gardener to find out that a bulb planter works great for planting seedlings, too, but Cheryl Coston of Fair-dealing, Missouri, has a few tips of her own to make it work even better. First, she says, it's worthwhile to buy the kind of bulb planter that extracts the soil when you squeeze the handle; that way, you don't have to bend. If you're planting into plastic mulch, file the edge of the bulb planter to make it sharper; then you can cut through the plastic and dig the hole with one twisting stroke. And if you've ever used a bulb planter in clay soil,

ON HAND: Chopsticks

TURN THEM INTO: Dibble for small seedlings

HOW TO DO IT: Use a single chopstick to poke seed holes when sowing seeds or to prick out seedlings when transplanting. Alison Kenny, a backyard gardener who also makes luscious skin creams and lotions in her Maryland kitchen, adds that chopsticks are great disposable "spoons" for messy stirring jobs, like beeswax and oils.

you know that it leaves the sides of the hole compacted and slick, which roots will find difficult to penetrate. "My solution is to carry an old dinner fork with me," Coston says. "A couple of slashing jabs at the sides of the hole loosen the soil just fine."

JUST-RIGHT SHOVEL I

Just about every gardener has a tool they wouldn't be without, and extension horticulture agent Sydney Park Brown is no exception.

When she heads toward her perennial beds, she's usually carrying her favorite implement: an irrigation shovel (also known as a trenching shovel). No, Park Brown has no need to dig water ditches in her Tampa, Florida, garden; she just finds this short-handled, narrow-bladed shovel ideally suited for a woman. Its long, narrow blade is perfect for controlling the size of the holes she digs, and because the blade doesn't hold much soil, it never gets too heavy to lift. The D-shaped handle and short shaft give her just enough leverage to transplant perennials or root up weeds and yet still allow her to work easily in a small space.

JUST-RIGHT SHOVEL II

The gracefully curved raised beds in Bruce Gleeman's backyard provide an abundance of fresh flowers and herbs to enhance many of his culinary creations. To tend his diverse backyard plot, this Philadelphia-based baker and caterer relies on one garden tool over all others—a war-surplus entrenching tool. Gleeman finds this compact shovel excellent for getting into tight spaces as he works his compost-enriched loam. The spade head folds and locks in different positions, so he can also use this tool as a lightweight pick for busting up clods or removing a stray tree root. Plus, when folded, it takes up little room in his crowded tool shed.

FAKE FLOWERS MARK THE SPOT

Linda Howard, a home gardener from Evansville, Indiana, was new to gardening when she hit upon an idea for marking planting spots that also makes her garden look pretty. "In the spring, I keep an eye out for artificial flowers at yard sales, the kind with a stiff wire single stem. I use them to mark where I've planted daffodils and other bulbs, and in the vegetable garden, I use them at both ends of the row. So I don't forget what I planted there, I poke the wire through the seed packet to keep it in place. My flowers are easy to spot at a glance, so even the kids don't go trampling the rows I've planted."

The fake flowers stay in place through wind and rain. When the plants are up and growing, Howard pulls out the fake flowers, snips off the wire stems to use as twist-ties in the garden, and tosses out the faded blooms.

It's Time for Daffodils

Daffodil lover Sally Roth of New Harmony, Indiana, often stops at other people's gardens to ask about unusual varieties that catch her eye. Yet by the time daffodil-planting time rolls around, she says, "I've either forgotten the name or lost the paper I'd written it on, or even worse, I've forgotten to order the bulbs and the mail-order companies have sold out."

"I've tried pinning my notes to a bulletin board and sticking them on the refrigerator, but that doesn't work either. By fall, I'm so used to seeing that important reminder that I never even notice it," she says. So she turned to a thoroughly low-tech gadget—the calendar on her kitchen wall.

"In April, when I have the name of a new daffodil I want to try, I flip to the August page—when it's time to start buying daffodils—and make a note on any date, saying 'Buy daffodil 'Halesa', or whatever it is I want to try." Roth says she also jots down a few words about good companion plants and what she likes about the flower: its color, height, fragrance, and overall look, in case her landscaping designs have changed by the time it's time to order.

This reminder system works well for other plants whose planting time is different than

ON HAND: Plastic-foam packing peanuts

TURN THEM INTO: Pot drainage assistant

HOW TO DO IT: Layer plastic-foam packing peanuts about 1 inch thick in the bottom of small pots, or up to 3 inches deep in larger pots, for perfect drainage with no weight. It's especially good for hanging containers, says Irv Breber of Bensalem, Pennsylvania.

"I've also tilled them 7 to 8 inches deep into hard-packed soil areas where nothing much would grow, which increased the drainage enough to turn the soil into a successful planting area."

bloom time, says Roth, who uses the same system to make note of bearded irises and daylilies she likes.

LITTLE RED WAGON IS A BIG HELP

"My 3-year-old, Erica, isn't very good at weeding the garden or planting seeds," says Gretel Hartman of the Boston area, "but she does love to help. So I give her things that she can handle, and that's where her little red wagon comes in handy. It's great for moving around the small pots of plants I start indoors or buy at the garden center, or for moving transplants."

In fact, says Hartman, the wagon is so useful that she has adopted it even when Erica isn't helping. She uses it to hold weeds for transport to the compost pile, and she has even used it to give away extra bearded irises, sundrops (*Oenothera* sp.), mint, and other prolific growers, as well as her extra ripe tomatoes and zucchini. The wagon is narrower than her wheelbarrow, she notes, so it fits in tight quarters in the garden without damaging nearby plants.

"The first time I used it as a plant stand, I piled it with irises when I thinned out my beds and put a sign on it that said 'Free plants—please help yourself!'" says Hartman. The freebies were snapped up within a couple of hours by passersby in the neighborhood, who tell Hartman that they can't wait for the next appearance of the little red wagon.

ON HAND: Plastic pots
TURN THEM INTO: Handy scoops
HOW TO DO IT: "Save all your sturdy 3-, 4-, and 6-inch plastic pots. When you aren't using them for repotting, they make excellent scoops for potting soil, mulch, pet food, and bird seed," says Linda Harris of Fulton, Kentucky. Simply wash and dry them, and stick a little tape over the holes to keep scoop from leaking.

PERFECT POTTING TABLE

If you have an old dresser, sideboard, or vanity, then you have an instant potting table. All you have to do is set the piece of furniture outside. The drawers make great storage and the top is a perfect surface for puttering with plants or stacking pots. If the design permits, add hooks for hanging hand tools.

PVC MARKS THE SPOT

Can't figure out a use for those short pieces of PVC pipe? Turn them into planting markers. Push pipe pieces into flowerbeds to mark locations of dormant bulbs or wildflowers, or use them as row markers in the vegetable garden.

Build It!

PLANTING COMPASS

If you want to plant your seedlings the exact same space apart, Jeff Ball's garden compass may be just the gadget you need. Ball, a garden writer from West Chester, Pennsylvania, says it was his idea and his father's ability to manufacture it. "This compass is modeled on the compasses we used in grade school to draw circles on the blackboard," says Ball. My father and I devised it to be used when planting a vegetable garden with the intensive planting method. We wanted to place each plant exactly within its tolerance in terms of distance from another plant in 360 degrees of direction. It's also handy when you simply need to plant 20 seedlings 5 inches apart."

To make the compass, use a couple pieces of scrap wood. Hardwood like oak or maple will last longer, but use whatever you have on hand. You can buy threaded rod already cut, or you can simply hacksaw the head off a machine bolt.

Materials

Two $1\frac{1}{2} \times 18$-inch pieces of $\frac{1}{2}$-inch-thick hardwood

$1\frac{1}{2}$-inch length of $\frac{1}{4}$-inch threaded rod

Two washers for $\frac{1}{4}$-inch bolt

Two $\frac{1}{4}$-inch wing nuts

Band saw, saber saw, or handsaw

Drill

WASHER

THREADED ROD

WING NUT

DIRECTIONS

1. Cut the wood to about 18-inches long. Make a pattern for a long, tapered shape, based on the illustration at left. Mark the pattern on each piece of wood and cut to shape. (A band saw or saber saw would be helpful, but a handsaw will work as well.)

2. Cut the narrow ends to form a point on each piece, round the corners on the thicker end of each piece, and sand the rough edges.

3. Drill a $\frac{1}{4}$-inch hole $\frac{3}{4}$ inch from the rounded ends of each piece.

4. Thread the rod through the two wood strips and attach with a washer and wing nut on each side. Tighten the nuts to hold the compass securely. Loosen the nuts to adjust the angle as needed.

ON HAND: Broken metal or plastic miniblinds

TURN THEM INTO: Plant labels

HOW TO DO IT: Sally Cummings of Albany, New York, clips labels to length with a sturdy scissors, making one end of the label pointed. Then she uses a permanent marker or a laundry marker to write pertinent information on the label.

You can easily write notes on them with a marking pen.

HERE'S THE SCOOP

Here's a gadget that comes in handy when you need a scoop of potting soil or peat moss. All you need to make your own is a clean, empty plastic bottle with a handle and a pair of craft or kitchen scissors, says Judy Glattstein of Frenchtown, New Jersey. Just lay the bottle on its side, with the handle on top. Make a partial cut as for a funnel, more than one-third but somewhat less than one-half the circumference of the bottle, starting just below the handle. Then, from each end of that cut, make an angled cut along the body of the cylinder down to the base, narrowing gradually toward the base. Join the cuts just before you reach the bottom of the bottle, as shown, to make a handy, all-purpose scoop.

GET THE SCOOP ON POTTING SOIL BY MAKING A SOIL SCOOP OUT OF A CLEAN PLASTIC BOTTLE.

CARPET MAGIC

Try a little carpet in your garden. Gardener Sally Roth of New Harmony, Indiana, author of *Attracting Birds to Your Backyard*, doesn't have raised beds, so she uses carpet samples for garden seats, which give her a comfy seat at ground level. "They keep the seat of my jeans clean and dry," she says, "and make it possible for me to work in my garden even right after a rain." Roth asks at carpet stores for outdated samples.

Build It!

HOLDING BED FOR POTTED PLANTS

Have you ever gone plant shopping and brought home lots of great treasures, only to realize you don't have a place ready for them in the garden? Ernest Heintzelman of Kempton, Pennsylvania, certainly knows what that's like! He was lucky enough to snap up 12 pine seedlings for only $5, but he needed time to prepare a good planting site for them. Heintzelman knew that keeping all those small pots upright and watered could be a real challenge, so he decided to create a holding bed where they would be safe until he was ready to plant them.

Heintzelman built a simple frame from scrap lumber, and then filled it with chipped hardwood mulch (free from many local townships) and sunk his potted trees to their rims in the mulch. The mulch drains well but also reduces water loss from evaporation, so the pots don't need frequent watering. "You can hold most woody plants in a nursery for several years, with periodic feedings of fish emulsion or compost tea," he says.

Materials

16 feet of 1 × 8 or 2 × 8 lumber

12 penny nails (or 2- to 3-inch galvanized deck screws)

Potted seedlings

Hardwood mulch

Circular saw or handsaw

Hammer or a cordless drill with both drill-bit and driver attachments

Framing square or measuring tape

DIRECTIONS

1. Cut the lumber into four 4-foot sections using a circular saw or handsaw. (If you want a smaller or larger bed, adjust the lengths accordingly.)

2. Nail each corner together with two to four nails, or drill pilot holes with a cordless drill, and then use a driver attachment to drive in galvanized deck screws. Make sure the corners are square with a framing square, or measure across the diagonals (they should be equal).

3. Position the nursery frame in an out-of-the-way spot, set in your potted plants, and then fill in around them with mulch.

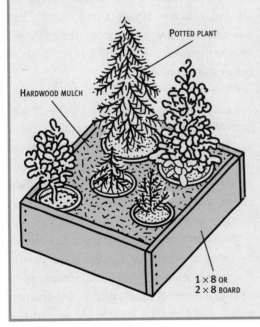

POTTED PLANT

HARDWOOD MULCH

1 × 8 OR 2 × 8 BOARD

ON HAND: A plastic kitty litter jug

TURN IT INTO: Plant markers

HOW TO DO IT: Using a pair of heavy-duty scissors, cut out strips of jug the length and width you need. Use a permanent marker to write on them.

WALK THE PLANK!

Donna Armstrong of Harleysville, Pennsylvania, remarks, "The old ways are often the best!" She and others who garden at Heckler Plains Farmstead, an 18th-century German kitchen garden located in Harleysville, use long wooden planks, just as their historical counterparts did years ago. Laying the plank over a raised bed (the hallmark of the kitchen garden) creates a wonderful, clean platform from which to plant, weed, or cultivate. The edge of the plank is an excellent marker for sowing precise, straight rows, too. Plank criteria? Something that is long enough to lay on top of the raised bed. After all, the gardeners of yore would have recycled what was available. So don't sweat dimensions.

FLATWARE FOR YOUR FLOWERS

Sturdy plastic flatware is ideal for labeling outdoor plantings. Use a #2 pencil to write information on the blade of the knife or bowl of the spoon—ink (even from indelible markers) doesn't usually hold up. Push the flatware handle into the soil until only the top inch of the utensil is showing. Rest assured the marker will be there next spring to warn you before digging into lilies, hibiscus, and other late-emerging perennials! To make shorter labels for small pots, snip plastic flatware in half.

DISHPANS FOR DAYLILIES

Try a daylily dishpan trick to keep yourself organized at planting time, says teenager David Roth-Mark of New Harmony, Indiana. Roth-Mark has been a daylily enthusiast since he planted his first garden. At first he planted a jumble of colors and heights, but now that he's developing more design sense, he often moves the plants around to get a better combination.

"The trouble is, unless they're blooming, you can't tell one daylily from another," says Roth-Mark. He depends on plant markers to keep the names straight in his garden, but when it's time to transplant, he commonly ends up with a pile of unidentified plants, no matter how hard he tries to remember what's what.

Roth-Mark has solved his plant ID dilemma by using inexpensive light-colored plastic dishpans to hold daylilies for transplanting. "I write the name of the daylily on the dishpan with a black marker before I even put the

Build It!

A Very Able Label

Midwestern winters are tough on a lot of things—people, animals, and even plant labels. Frost heaves them out of the ground and severe weather beats off any writing on them in just a few months.

So Lee and Ruth White of Postville, Iowa, have come up with a super label that handles even what the harshest weather dishes up.

Materials

Piece of 1 × 3-inch wood, ½ inch thick

Heavy-duty aluminum foil

Drill

12-inch length #9 galvanized wire

Heavy-duty stapler and staples

Ballpoint pen

Permanent marker (optional)

Directions

1. Cut the wood to size, and drill a hole in the center near the top.

2. Cut the foil to fit the front of the wood, and staple it in place.

3. Use a ballpoint pen to write the plant name on the foil, pressing firmly. If desired, trace over the writing with a permanent marker.

4. Loop the wire through the hole as shown.

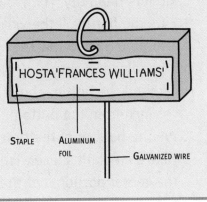

STAPLE ALUMINUM FOIL GALVANIZED WIRE

HOSTA 'FRANCES WILLIAMS'

plants in," he says. "The dishpan makes it easy to cart the plants around, it holds them securely, and, with a little water in the bottom, it keeps them fresh until I can get them into the ground."

CLASSY LABELS

Fancy copper plant labels look great, but they cost a fortune and are often so undersize that they give you just an inch or two to insert them into the soil. Make your own elegant copper labels by purchasing sheets of thin copper at a crafts store. Just cut into the size and shape desired with a pair of craft or kitchen scissors. Label by pressing firmly with a dull pencil.

EXTRA-LARGE LABELS

Most store-bought plant labels are too narrow to hold much more than a plant's name. That can be a problem if you want to include additional information for vegetable crops,

ON HAND: Bleach bottle

TURN IT INTO: Plant marking stakes and plant saucer

HOW TO DO IT: Lois Stringer of Bellefonte, Pennsylvania, rinses empty bleach bottles and lets them dry. Then she cuts the bottle all the way around, just below the handle, and cuts again around the bottle, about ½ inch from the bottom. Save the bottom of the bottle to use as a plant saucer. From the center portion, cut the circle apart so you can flatten out into a panel. (You may need to roll in the opposite direction of how it's curved to get it to lie flat.) Cut it across the short width to make ¾-inch strips for plant markers, which take permanent marker or crayon very well.

such as planting date, expected harvest date, and so on. Frustrated by narrow commercial plant labels, Cheryl Coston of Fairdealing, Missouri, came up with a way to make extra-large labels. "First, I bought an inexpensive package of wooden skewers," she says. "They were about 12 inches long, with 20 in a package for $1. Then I stuck them in a piece of plastic foam and spray painted them white." That created attractive and durable stakes.

For the labels themselves, Coston cut 4 × 6-inch rectangles from a white bleach bottle, made five evenly spaced, horizontal slits across each one, and wove the skewers through them. She uses a Sharpie pen to write all the notes she needs to make on the rectangles and sets them out in the garden. "I thought they might look tacky but figured they would do until I could figure out an alternative," Coston says. "But they don't look tacky or like bleach bottles at all, and I'm still using them. Best of all, I can read them without even bending over!"

COLOR THEM PRETTY, COLOR THEM RIGHT

Raising seedlings is a passion for Caroline Whitenack of Doylestown, Pennsylvania. She raises hundreds of flower seedlings every year to plant her dozen different gardens and local church gardens and to supply neighbors and family with plants.

To keep her seedlings identified so they don't get mixed up, she buys 12-inch plastic stakes and cuts them into thirds, then uses stick-on color dots in various colors (available in office-supply stores) to color-code the seedlings. She uses the color-coding system for the seedlings until they are transplanted into their final setting. Whitenack says she never has unwelcome surprises when the plants bloom!

Glue Stick Saves Seeds at Planting Time

Have you ever spilled the excess seed from a seed packet all over a garden bed because the seed packet flap just wouldn't stay shut? Sometimes you don't want to plant a whole packet of lettuce, beans, or annual flowers at one time, but it's a problem to keep the opened seed packets securely shut.

"Some seeds don't come in resealable packets, and the ones that do often lose their stickiness after being opened a few times," observes gardener Cheryl Coston of Fairdealing, Missouri. "So I learned to carry a restickable-type glue stick along in my planting tote. The glue stick works perfectly for creating a good sticky seal on a seed packet flap."

Glue sticks are available at discount stores and office supply stores, and they cost less than $2.

Recycle It!

ON HAND: Plastic foam meat trays

TURN THEM INTO: Foolproof tomato cage labels

HOW TO DO IT: It's impossible to find labels stuck in the ground once tomato vines sprawl. Instead, cut strips of plastic foam and punch a hole in one corner of each strip with a hole puncher. Write the ID on the label, then thread a twist-tie through the hole, and attach the label to the top of tomato cage where it's easily visible.

Plant Protectors

Half of the gardening battle is over: Your seeds have finally sprouted! Now is the ideal time to protect your plants from the will of the weather. This section will suggest ways to keep your plants warm and safe without having to depend upon expensive commercial products.

BULB DEFENDER

City dwellers often discover their freshly planted bulbs dug up and scattered about. Is the culprit a jealous neighbor? A pesky pooch? "It's most likely squirrels," says Judy Glattstein, author of *Flowering Bulbs for Dummies* and world-renowned bulb lecturer. "Squirrels may think that light, fluffy soil means something tasty has been buried by another squirrel and will dig up (but not eat) your tulips and daffodils." To keep these critters from excavating your bulb beds, Glattstein recommends dropping an old window screen or short lengths of thorny rose or bramble branches over the site. Once the ground firms up or freezes, you can remove these defenses and wait for your spring show.

TOMATO PROTECTION

Laurie Kendrick of Hooper, Utah, protects tender tomato seedlings with pieces of 4-inch-wide PVC pipe cut into 12- to 14-inch lengths. After she has planted the seedlings, she carefully puts a piece of PVC pipe over the top of each one and pushes it into the ground. Laurie leaves the PVC on all growing season to protect the tomatoes from cutworms and to provide support.

KEEP CUTWORMS FROM DAMAGING YOUR TOMATOES AND SUPPORT THE PLANTS AT THE SAME TIME.

WALL OF PLASTIC

Vincent Norris of State College, Pennsylvania, has invented his own tomato plant protectors that he says outperform commercial water-filled cloches. All it takes to protect a plant from cold weather is a 1-gallon plastic milk jug and an empty 6-gallon plastic bucket (check with local contractors for drywall buckets).

Norris plants his tomatoes as soon as the morning soil temperature reaches 55°F. (That's still several weeks before the last frost date in his area.) He places a water-filled jug next to each plant at planting time. Then every evening, he inverts a bucket over each tomato plant and the jug beside it. "The water in the jug keeps the temperature inside the bucket well above the outside air temperature." he says. "By the time the tomato plants become too large to fit inside a bucket, they no longer need the covers," he says. "I've never lost a single tomato plant to frost," he adds.

PLANT PROTECTION CUBED

Cool-climate gardeners know the value of water-filled containers for insulating their vegetable crops from the cold. Kelly Winterton of Mountain Green, Utah, works in a high-volume, photo-finishing lab and has access to used 4- and 5-gallon, flexible, collapsible plastic containers in which the photo chemicals are shipped. (He calls them "cubitainers.") Winterton recognized their garden potential and turned them into season extenders.

"I rinse the cubitainers out well," he explains, "and then fill them with water and place them around plants that are sensitive to cold. They hold much more water than

ON HAND: Odd pieces of PVC pipe and an old bedsheet

TURN THEM INTO: Shade cover for transplants

HOW TO DO IT: Stick pipe pieces into the ground among plants and spread the sheet over them. Weight the corners with bricks.

similar commercial products and the plants never outgrow them. I leave them in place all growing season," Winterton continues. "In the summer, they tend to moderate the extreme heat, so they work well with plants that need a little relief from the heat in the middle of the day, such as broccoli and cauliflower. When the cooler weather of the fall arrives, the cubitainers are still there, doing their job. I can easily overwinter my cole crops here in Zone 4. And as soon as the snow melts, they resume growing to give me a spring crop way before the cabbageworms become active."

Winterton points out that because of their size, the cubitainers also serve as a mulch to moderate soil and air temperature. He suggests that you can enhance the insulating power of the cubitainers even more by covering them and the plant with floating row covers or ventilated clear plastic. The secret is volume and mass. "Getting 30 gallons of water around each plant makes all the difference in the world," Winterton says.

CLOCHE SECURITY FLAP

A lot of you probably cut the bottoms off of gallon milk jugs and place the jugs over plants as cloches. These individual plant shel-

ON HAND: Old sheets and mangled paper clips

TURN THEM INTO: Shade cover for transplants

HOW TO DO IT: Cover newly planted shrubs, perennials, and other transplants by cutting a section of sheet to drape over the tops and sides of the plant. If necessary, secure the cloth to the soil by bending a few of the clips into U-pins. Remove after 1 or 2 days.

ters can speed early growth. Using them also helps prevent cool-season crops such as cabbage, cauliflower, and broccoli from going to seed prematurely. Only trouble is, the empty jugs are lightweight and not very secure. There's a simple way to correct the problem: Instead of cutting the entire bottom from the jug, make a large flap by cutting along three sides of the bottom. Then bend the flap out 180 degrees and cover it with soil or large rocks to hold the jug in place. What a simple solution!

FIG PROTECTION

If you're growing fig trees anywhere cooler than Zone 7, you have to nurse the trees through the winter, and that can be a big job. "I used to wrap my fig tree with burlap," says Joseph Schlien of Baltimore, Maryland, "but it was a lot of work, and the wraps kept coming apart." Since then, he has found the perfect wrap: tubular foam insulation that slips over water pipes. Schlien has found that it fits perfectly over the trunk and branches of his fig tree! He simply slips it over and tapes it with electrical black tape. He bought all he needed for $5 and says he can use it over and over again, year after year.

HOMEMADE HOT HOUSE

"I'm a tomato fanatic!" says Linda Monier of Olive Branch, Mississippi. "And I want them early!" Monier makes the most of her growing season by creating a special solar-heated bed for her tomatoes. About 6 weeks before last frost—that's April 15 in her area—she covers a 4 by 8-foot bed with black plastic mulch and then sinks 6- to 7-foot-tall rebar stakes

1 or 2 feet deep every 30 inches or so just outside the long edges of the bed. When the last frost date has passed, she digs a planting hole to the inside of each stake and plants her tomatoes.

To create a low-tech drip-watering system, she cuts off the bottom of 2-liter soda bottles, drills a couple of holes in each lid with a cordless drill, and then buries them about 6 inches deep, top-end down—one beside each plant. "When I need to water, I just fill up the upside-down bottles," she says.

Even in her southern garden, late spring can throw in a few chilly days, so Monier has come up with some clever insulation ideas to keep her tomato seedlings warm and cozy. "I take empty milk jugs, fill them with water, and place them around the plants," she says. "I use as many milk jugs as will fit into the bed without crowding the plants too much—and that's a lot! Then I take 4-mil-thick clear plastic sheeting and wrap it around the stakes on the outside, completely enclosing the bed in a mini greenhouse." (The top is left open to avoid overheating.) "The plants get off to a great start!" Monier claims.

Once the days are dependably warm and night temperatures remain at least 60°F, she removes the clear plastic. And when it gets really hot, she removes the water jugs and covers the black plastic with straw to keep the roots from cooking. "I have tomatoes by June 1 every year!" she says.

KEEPING KITTY IN

Most of us put up fences to keep critters—rabbits, raccoons, and deer—out of our yards. But some of us need fences to keep critters—

ON HAND: Half-gallon plastic juice bottles

TURN THEM INTO: Tomato plant insulators

HOW TO DO IT: After planting tomato seedlings, surround each one with six juice bottles filled with water, and then wrap the whole thing in bubble wrap. The bottles insulate the plants during cold nights. As warmer weather arrives, unwrap the bubble wrap and remove the bottles.

especially our feline friends—in, to keep them safe and prevent them from digging in our neighbors' yards.

Cats, of course, are climbers, so it takes a little ingenuity to build a fence to contain them. Nancy Milligan of Lemon Grove, California, has found the answer. She simply installed V-shaped, 45-degree brackets near the top along the inside of the existing 6-foot-tall fence that surrounded her yard. (To make these brackets, she purchased metal shelving brackets and bent them from a 90-degree angle to a 45-degree angle. The brackets already have holes in them, so it's easy to attach them to a wooden fence using ½-inch screws.) Milligan then fastened a long strip of hardware cloth on top of the brackets with twist ties or wire to make an impenetrable cat barrier. Milligan points out that plastic netting or wooden lattice would also do the trick.

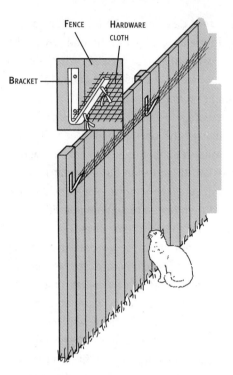

KEEP YOUR CAT IN YOUR YARD—AND OUT OF THE NEIGHBORS'—WITH THIS SIMPLE HARDWARE-CLOTH BARRIER. BECAUSE IT ANGLES INWARD, KITTY CAN'T GET PAST IT.

ON HAND: 2-liter soda bottles

TURN THEM INTO: Plant protectors

HOW TO DO IT: Scrape the label from a 2-liter soda bottle using a utility knife or a single-edge razor, and then cut the base off the bottle. Lower the bottle over a small plant, and twist it into the soil. Remove the cap to ventilate during the day, and replace the cap at night.

RING AROUND THE TREE TRUNK

Ever drive up to your house just as the fellow who cuts your lawn was mowing down one of your newly planted saplings? Randy Myer of Hastings, New York, did and he wasn't amused. So he invented a perforated plastic tree collar that snaps around a young tree. As the trunk grows, the diaphragm opening expands to fit it, just as a camera lens opens to let in more light. The plastic surface is easy to conceal with mulch, thousands of tiny holes let plenty of water through to the roots, and best of all, the raised rim keeps lawn mowers at bay. (See "Resources" on page 144 for ordering information.)

PROTECT YOUR TREE'S BARK FROM LAWN MOWER BITES WITH THIS TREE COLLAR FASHIONED FROM THE BOTTOM PART OF A PLASTIC NURSERY POT.

If you're a do-it-yourselfer at heart, you can make a trunk protector from a 5-gallon or larger plastic nursery pot. Simply slice off the bottom, cutting through the container about 1 inch from the bottom edge. With a hammer and nail, poke holes in the bottom surface—the more the merrier. Then cut a hole with a craft scissors or utility knife in the center that's big enough to accommodate your sapling's trunk with a few inches to spare. Make a slit from the hole to the outer edge so the collar will open, slip it in place around the tree, and

ON HAND: Sheer white window curtains

TURN THEM INTO: Row covers

HOW TO DO IT: Drape old curtains over garden plants to protect them from insects or light frosts. They work great and hold up better than expensive spun garden fabrics. You can even throw them in the washer if needed!

disguise the plastic surface with mulch. Keep an eye on the collar as your tree grows and remove it before the fit gets snug. By then, your tree should be big enough to catch someone's attention before it's too late.

Seed-Starting Stuff

What do film canisters, hoes, rulers, forks, and cardboard toilet-paper rolls have in common? With a little gardening imagination and effort, they can make seed starting a snap. In the next few pages, you'll learn how to make homemade flat covers, planting boxes, mini greenhouses, and coldframes for your next seed-starting projects.

BENCHMARKED SEED STORAGE

"Seeds from some trees and wildflowers germinate better when they get a good winter chill, but I don't like to put messy seeds planted in soil in my refrigerator," says gardener Barbara Pleasant, who's trying to reforest several acres of land in Alabama with native plant seedlings. Instead, Pleasant uses her outdoor potting bench as a storage site for seeds that need a cold treatment. After collecting the seeds, she sticks them in a small paper envelope. Then she tucks the envelope into a margarine tub filled with damp potting soil. She uses a marker to label the lid of the container about the contents. Then she stashes the containers in the pile of leaves that accumulates under her potting bench.

"By February, when I'm ready to plant the seeds in flats, they think they've been through winter. Sometimes they're already beginning to sprout when I take them out of the tubs," Pleasant says.

ARTISTIC FLAT COVERS

Most seeds crave light to help them germinate, but verbenas and some other flowers like to sprout in the dark. "When I sow flats of flower seeds that like to germinate in darkness, I cover them with pieces of illustration board cut slightly larger than the flats," says Alabama gardener Barbara Pleasant. "I use bricks to hold the board in place. The board keeps things dark and moist. Heavy cardboard will work, too, but it isn't as durable as illustration board," Pleasant says. You can buy illustration board at art-supply stores.

PLANT-IN-A-BOX

Each year, Delores and Dave Johnson of Golden Valley, Minnesota, start about 8,000 plants from seed—with no greenhouse. (Saying they know how to start seeds efficiently is an understatement.) How do they do it?

Dave says he likes to speed the process by not using little flats. Instead, he has built a large planting box (line with galvanized metal) about 3 × 2 feet and 4 to 6 inches deep. (You could make yours any dimensions you want.) He puts a layer of crushed rock on the bottom, topped by a little sand. The top 2 inches are filled with seed-starting mix. He hangs a cool, white four-bulb fluorescent light about 4 inches above the planting box.

You could plant seeds in the box just as it is, but Dave likes to further refine the process by cutting 2 × 4-inch dividers from strips of galvanized metal for his 3 × 2-foot box. He inserts those into the soil about 1 or 2 inches, just enough to keep the seedlings neatly apart.

Then Dave sows the seeds. He can get up to 60 different types of seeds in his box. And because of its size, the box has a more stable temperature and retains moisture better than smaller containers.

ON HAND: A small plastic fork

TURN IT INTO: A transplanting tool for small seedlings

HOW TO DO IT: Break off the two outside prongs of the fork, leaving just two prongs. Slip the tines around an individual seedling and carefully lever it out of the seed-starting tray, roots and all.

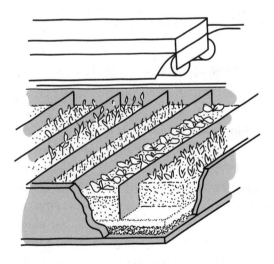

MAXIMIZE LIMITED SPACE WITH THIS SEED-STARTING PLANTING BED.

RULE IT OUT

Cut an old yardstick down to size—a tad shorter than the width of a seed tray, to be precise—and you're ready to fly through planting. Just fill the tray with your seed starting mix, level it off, and mark rows about 1½ inches apart with the cut ruler's edge. You can easily control the depth this way, and keep rows straight.

If you have, say, several varieties of tomato plants you wish to try this year, mark many short rows width-wise across the flat. Then plant the seeds, skipping a row between varieties (don't forget to label each variety!). This system gets the seeds off to a great start and makes transplanting easy.

ON HAND: Clear plastic clamshell containers (the kind you get salads in at delis)

TURN THEM INTO: A mini greenhouse for starting seeds

HOW TO DO IT: Just wash out the container, add your favorite seed-starting mix, and plant your seeds. Open container as needed to vent or water.

Cut paper towels into 1-inch-wide strips and squeeze the gelatin seed mixture onto the paper-towel strips, spacing seeds according to seed packet directions. Allow the strips to dry. Then roll them up loosely, and store for up to 2 days.

In the garden, unroll the seed strips in a furrow and cover with soil.

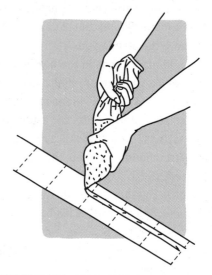

HOMEMADE SEED TAPE I

Seed tapes make sowing and spacing seeds in the garden easy and precise. The problem is pre-made tapes are expensive, and you can't always get your favorite varieties on a tape. The solution is to make your own—it's a fun activity for a rainy day when you can't get out in the garden.

You'll need one package of gelatin (any type), one resealable plastic bag, a roll of paper towels, and your seeds. Make the gelatin in a bowl according to package directions and allow it to cool but not set. Pour the seed into the bowl of cooled gelatin and mix thoroughly.

Cut a hole, just large enough for a single seed to fit through, in one corner of the bottom of a plastic bag. Spoon the gelatin and seed mixture into the bag.

SAVE MONEY—AND USE THE VARIETIES YOU LIKE BEST—BY MAKING YOUR OWN SEED TAPE INSTEAD OF BUYING A COMMERCIAL ONE.

HOMEMADE SEED TAPE II

Here's a variation on the theme of making your own seed tapes. Instead of using gelatin, make a thick paste of flour and water (experiment to get the right consistency) to hold the seeds in place. Roll the paste into pea-size balls, space them out to the appropriate distance on a 1-inch-wide strip of newspaper or paper towel, and then press them flat to hold them in place. Next, push a single seed into each spot of paste. After the paste dries, you can plant the entire "tape" in the garden.

Homemade Seed Tape III

Toilet paper and glue are the basis of yet another gardener's method for making seed tape. Pat Patterson of Eugene, Oregon, finds that making her own seed tapes is a great winter-gardening activity. Patterson uses single-layer toilet paper and white glue to make the tape. She unrolls the paper and squeezes out two or more lines of glue on it. Then she places the seeds on the glue, spaced according to the seed packet directions. (Use a moistened toothpick or tweezers for tiny seed that are hard to hold.)

Pat lets the tape dry thoroughly, and then rolls it up and labels it until planting time. (When planting, be sure to cover the paper completely so it doesn't wick moisture.)

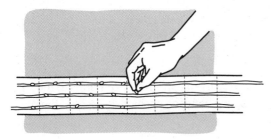

A LITTLE GLUE AND SOME TOILET PAPER GO A LONG WAY WHEN MAKING A SEED TAPE.

Waterbed Germinator

Starting seeds indoors can save you plenty of dollars compared to buying plants at the garden center, but unless you keep the seeds warm enough, poor germination can be a problem. Commercial seed-starting mats are an option, but they can be expensive, too. For an inexpensive substitute that will provide *plenty* of well-heated space for seed starting, check yard sales and want ads for a single-size, waterbed mattress. To use the mattress for

ON HAND: Butcher's twine, kite string, or cotton yarn

TURN IT INTO: Seed-starting tape

HOW TO DO IT: Head out to the garden armed with a pail of water, a 7- to 8-inch length of twine, seeds, and some old newspaper. Put the twine in the pail, and while it soaks, dig your planting furrow. By the time you do that, the twine should be saturated. Then sprinkle a row of seeds the same length on a sheet of the newspaper. Dip the twine in the seeds and plant the whole thing. As the seedlings germinate, the twine will degrade, giving a bit of organic matter to the soil. Says Sunnyvale, California, Master Gardener Dagmar Cechanek, "It's great for those almost-invisible seeds like carrots, lettuce, or nigella. I find it much easier than the classic method of mixing them with sand."

Build It!

CUSTOMIZED HOOP COLDFRAME

Professional gardener Gary Prochaska of Ames, Iowa, makes coldframes that fit over planting beds and crop rows using bits and pieces of materials he has around the garage. He customizes them for a wide variety of shapes and erects some long *after* the crop is planted. Prochaska, for example, uses his to extend the harvest of spinach, radishes, and turnips.

Materials

At least six 12-inch lengths of 2-inch-diameter galvanized steel fence posts or similarly sized lengths of metal pipe

6-foot lengths of PVC flexible well pipe, one for each fence post

Two 2-foot stakes

Heavy string or cord

6-foot wide, 4-mil clear plastic

Bricks or stones

12-gauge wire in 12-inch lengths, bent to form a U

DIRECTIONS

1. Sink the fence posts or metal pipe into the ground, in a pattern that conforms to the cold-frame's outline. Leave no more than 3 feet of space between each post. Position the posts so the tops are 2 to 3 inches above the soil.

---

bottom heat, spread the mattress out on the floor in a spot where it won't be in your way, and fill it with water. Lay slats over the mattress, spaced about 1 foot apart, and place flats of seed trays or seed pots right on the slats. Once the seeds germinate, move the flats under lights.

A COOL SOLUTION FOR TRANSPLANT POTS

Next time you indulge in a pint or half-pint of ice cream, be sure to save the paper carton it came in: These containers make great pots for seedlings! Wash the ice cream container and lid thoroughly, and line the lid with aluminum foil. Poke a drainage hole in the bottom of the container, then place the lid under the container as a saucer. Fill the container with sterile potting soil to 1 inch below the top. Transplant one seedling into each container, then place them under lights until it's time to move them out to the garden. At transplanting time, remove the lid from the bottom and cut several slits in the bottom and sides, up to but not through the top rim. Plant the entire pot, leaving the top inch extending above ground for a built-in cutworm collar.

2. Insert the flexible well pipe into the posts, pushing the pipe down as far as possible.

3. Pound the stakes about halfway into the ground at each end of the frame. Tie string to one stake and then stretch and loop the string across the hoops as shown. Tie the string to the stake at the opposite end. This stabilizes the hoops. Repeat with two more lengths of string.

4. Place the plastic over the hoops and string, using bricks or stones to hold down any corners that may flap.

5. Place a piece of the 12-gauge U-shaped wire in front of each post. Then, to prevent the plastic from flapping stretch a length of string over the hoops and secure the string by tying each end to the U-shaped wire.

6. When you want to give the covered plants some ventilation, simply roll up the sides slightly, tucking the plastic under the outside strings secured with the U-shaped wires.

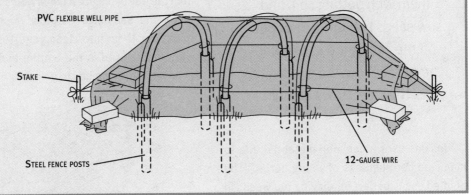

PVC FLEXIBLE WELL PIPE

STAKE

STEEL FENCE POSTS

12-GAUGE WIRE

SIMPLE SEED COLLECTORS

Cheryl Coston of Fairdealing, Missouri, used to use resealable plastic bags to collect seeds from her garden. It was never an easy process, though, trying to hold the bag open with one hand while collecting seeds with the other hand. Happily, she found a better alternative: Tupperware Hamburger Stackers. ("Finally a use for those things!" she says.) She carries a stack of them into the garden for collecting different types of seeds. And because one container serves as the lid for the next, there's no fumbling for separate covers.

MANICURE YOUR HERB SEEDLINGS

Herb gardener Pat Hoskins of Evansville, Indiana, likes to try new herbs from seed, but she found weeding and thinning the plants a painstaking chore, until she found just the right tool for the trick.

"None of my tools was small enough to lift out herb seedlings to get between the herbs to root out weeds," says Hoskins. "One day, I was walking around my yard with a nail file in hand, when I realized I had the perfect tool right in my fingers."

ON HAND: Toilet paper tubes

TURN THEM INTO: Seed-starting pots

HOW TO DO IT: Pack the tubes tightly into a seed-starting flat so that they stand upright. Fill them with potting soil, and sow seeds in them. Cut or peel off the cardboard at planting time, or set out the seedlings as they are, tubes and all.

Hoskins uses a common metal nail file to manicure her plantings of young herbs. "The pointed end is perfect for digging out weeds in those tight spaces. When I want to transplant herbs, I slip the file deep into the ground, round end first, to get below the roots and lift out the plant."

Hoskins gets double-duty out of her weeder, too. "When I'm done working in the herbs," she says, "I can clean my fingernails on the way to the house!"

EASY SEED-STARTING CARTONS

If your family drinks lots of milk or juice, chances are you have an ample supply of half-gallon cardboard cartons. S. D. H. Wilson of Stratford, Connecticut, has found a great gar-dening re-use for these containers: "They make fantastic seed-starting trays!" she says.

She cuts the cartons in half lengthwise, and then staples shut the pour-spout on the one half. "Then I poke a lot of holes in the bottom of each carton with an ice pick, fill them with damp starting medium, and plant my seeds." She fits about a half-dozen of the half-cartons on a tray and slips a large plastic bag—with the end open for air circulation—over them. (If you want to give the seeds some bottom heat to speed germination, set the tray on a wire cookie rack over a commercial seed-starting mat.)

When the seeds sprout in a carton, remove it from the tray and place it under florescent lights. When the seedlings outgrow their cartons, transplant them into clean yogurt containers with holes poked in the bottom and let them grow until they're ready to go into the garden.

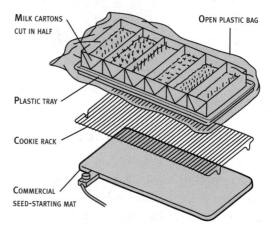

MILK CARTONS CUT IN HALF

OPEN PLASTIC BAG

PLASTIC TRAY

COOKIE RACK

COMMERCIAL SEED-STARTING MAT

DON'T THROW OUT THOSE EMPTY MILK CARTONS. INSTEAD, TURN THEM INTO SEED-STARTING TRAYS.

SODA BOTTLE GREENHOUSE

With a few cuts and a little taping, Wanda Thomas of Wright City, Missouri, transforms a 2-liter soda bottle into a mini greenhouse for starting seeds. Here's how: First remove the labels from the bottle, and then cut a 2-inch-wide section out of the middle of the bottle, leaving the top and bottom intact. Take the 2-inch section you removed and cut it in half to form two C-shaped strips of plastic. Tape the ends of each segment together to form two half-dollar-size, 2-inch-tall cylinders.

Use a nail to tap a few drainage holes in the bottom of the soda bottle. Turn the bottom right side up, add a 1-inch layer of potting soil, and then settle the two cylinders into the soil so they're right next to each other. (When you look down on them, they should form a figure eight, dividing the bottom of the bottle into four compartments.) Add enough potting soil to reach the top of the cylinders. Moisten the soil thoroughly, and sow the seeds.

Tape the top of the bottle to the bottom, and place the whole setup under plant lights on a windowsill with lots of bright but indirect natural light, or in a sheltered location outdoors. Remove the top half of the bottle when you need to water; leave it off when you are ready to harden-off the seedlings before moving them outdoors.

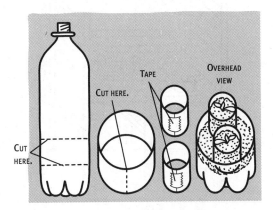

A COUPLE OF CUTS AND A FEW PIECES OF TAPE TRANSFORM A SIMPLE SODA BOTTLE INTO A SUPER SEED-STARTING SETUP.

Recycle It!

ON HAND: Plastic film canisters

TURN THEM INTO: Waterproof seed storage

HOW TO DO IT: Wash the plastic canisters with soap and warm water to make sure there are no residual chemicals and label them with masking tape. Make sure both the containers and your seeds are perfectly dry before you snap on the lids for storage.

KITTY'S CUSTOM TOMATO TRAYS

Seems like more and more things are packaged in plastic jugs, these days—even cat litter. That's the way Janelle Steckley of Sanford, Michigan, buys it, though she has always felt a little guilty about the plastic waste. "Even though I did put the jugs out in my recycling container when they were empty," she says, "it still somehow seemed wasteful." Not anymore, however. She has figured out how to reuse the containers by turning them into versatile plant pots for her seedlings. She just cuts off the top, pokes a few holes in the bottom for drainage using a nail, and then fills

ON HAND: Plastic film canisters

TURN THEM INTO: Space-saving seed stratifiers

HOW TO DO IT: If you have seeds that need to be chilled (stratified) before sowing, put each type in a separate canister along with enough damp, sterile potting soil to fill the container. Snap on the lid, label with masking tape, and place in the refrigerator to chill.

the container with potting soil. "The beauty of these containers is that you can make them as deep as you like," she says. "I like to transplant my tomato seedlings into deep pots after they grow their first true leaves. I bury them right up to their top leaves so the roots develop all the way up the stem." With their extra-deep root systems, her tomato plants get off to a great start in the garden!

SEEDS TAKE A SEAT

Those fancy seed-starting setups you see in catalogs are enticing—until you look at the price! "I really wanted one of those metal

shelving units with adjustable plant lights, but they sold for up to $600," recalls Pat Hall Borow of Decatur, Georgia. So about 5 years ago, she developed her own method. "It works great and is a whole lot cheaper than those commercial seed-starting units," she says.

Here's how to make your own: Place two ladder-back chairs facing one another, with the seats touching. Sow your seeds in two seed-starting trays with clear tops and drainage holes. Place the flats on a drip tray and set the tray across the seats. Take two fluorescent light sticks and tie a loop of string to the end of each stick. Then tie each end of the light stick to the bottom rung of the ladder-back chairs. (Use a slip knot or other temporary knot.) Now you have a light stick suspended just over each seed tray.

Keep the lids on the trays until your seeds have sprouted. When leaves begin to form, re-move the clear lids, and water and feed the seedlings as needed. As the seedlings grow, simply raise the light sticks by re-tying the strings on the next rung up.

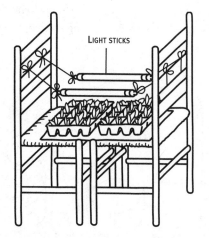

LIGHT STICKS

PULL UP A COUPLE OF LADDER-BACK CHAIRS, HANG TWO LIGHT STICKS IN BETWEEN THEM, AND YOU HAVE A LOW-COST, NO-FRILLS, SEED-STARTING SETUP!

Build It!

ADJUSTABLE GROW LIGHTS

Fluorescent shop-light fixtures are invaluable for indoor seed starting, but the short hanging chains they come with can make adjusting their height a challenge. Don Enge-bretson, a Minnesota Master Gardener and avid seed-starter, uses a handy pulley system to make raising and lowering his lights a snap! "This setup produces thick and bushy plants every time," says Engebretson.

Materials

Two U-hooks

2 clothesline pulleys

Two 10-foot clotheslines

4-foot fluorescent light fixture

2 S-hooks (usually supplied with fixture)

Two 1-foot lengths of light duty chain (usually supplied with fixture)

Heavy-duty alligator clips

Hammer or drill

DIRECTIONS

1. Install the U-hooks in your ceiling joists, spaced about 4 feet apart. Tap the end of each U-hook into the wood with a hammer (or predrill a hole if the wood is too hard), and then twist them until all the threads are in the wood.

2. Slip the ring on one pulley over the end of one U-hook. Repeat with the other pulley and U-hook.

3. Thread one end of each clothesline over each pulley. Tie one end of each clothesline to the end of a chain section.

4. Place the light fixture on the floor (if your seedlings will be sitting on the floor) or on your seed-starting bench. Hook one end of an S-hook onto the free end of the chain, and hook the other end of each S-hook onto the back of the fluorescent fixture.

5. Pull down on the free end of each clothesline to raise the light. Use the alligator clips to hold the ropes together when the lights are at the height you want (usually about 4 inches above the tops of the seedlings).

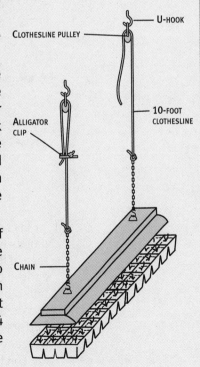

U-HOOK

CLOTHESLINE PULLEY

10-FOOT CLOTHESLINE

ALLIGATOR CLIP

CHAIN

Build It!

A Pallet-Table Plant Bench

After Lisa Anne Haynes and her husband finished building a greenhouse for their Mahomet, Illinois, garden, they needed to furnish it with sturdy benches and tables to hold flats of seedlings and potted plants. Rather than buying benches, the Hayneses found a way to beat that expense by building plant benches out of wooden pallets. Those ubiquitous pallets are easy to come by, of course, and turning them into benches turned out to be a simple task, too.

Materials

Used pallet

2 × 4, cut into four 3-foot lengths

Galvanized nails

Hammer

Saw

Directions

1. Lay the pallet down flat on a work surface and nail one 3-foot-long 2 × 4 leg to each corner of the pallet, perpendicular to the pallet.

2. Depending on the construction of the pallet, you may need to cut off the ends of the bottom deck boards at the corner so the legs can butt against the main pallet skids. (See below for details.)

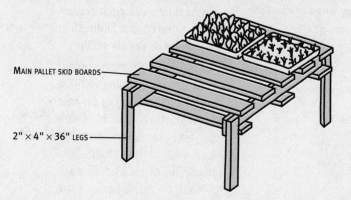

MAIN PALLET SKID BOARDS

2" × 4" × 36" LEGS

Lisa doesn't worry about the water that drips through the pallets when she waters her plants. In fact, she takes advantage of it by growing shiitake logs under the tables. However, early in the season, when she uses the benches as propagation tables, she covers the surface of the pallets with 3-mil-thick plastic, and places an electric space heater to provide bottom heat. After sowing her seed flats, she covers them with another sheet of plastic (over a bamboo frame) to keep the soil toasty and to encourage the seeds to pop up.

Mini Shade House

When she has to harden-off a lot of seedlings, Caroline Whitenack of Doylestown, Pennsylvania, creates a temporary shade house in miniature. She builds four pillars by stacking three plastic milk crates for each pillar. Then, she uses four 2 × 4s to create a frame, using the milk crate pillars as the corners. Nail the 2 × 4s together. (The frame could be any size, and you can use whatever size 2 × 4 scrap pieces you have on hand.)

After Whitenack lays out the frame, she drapes plastic window screening over the top of the frame and uses a staple gun to attach the screening to the wooden frame. Allow the screening to extend almost down to the ground.

This mini shade house provides a large, sheltered area for flats of plants. "This works wonderfully for shading a large amount of tender seedlings for several days to a week. When that group is ready for transplanting, I bring out more plants to harden off," says Whitenack. When she's finished using the shade house, she just dismantles it and either uses the parts for something else or stores them away.

No More Smashed Seedlings

Covering a seed-starting tray with plastic is a great way to provide emerging seedlings with a humid environment. Problem is, how do you keep the plastic off the seedlings? Lynn MacMahon, a gardener from Flushing, New York, came up with this resourceful way.

Heat an ice pick over the flame on a gas stove, and then use the pick to punch six holes in a plastic seed flat. (Wear heavy leather gloves while you do this to protect yourself from burns.) Punch one hole in each corner

ON HAND: Paper cups

TURN THEM INTO: Seed-starting containers

HOW TO DO IT: For an inexpensive alternative to peat or plastic pots, use small paper cups for indoor sowing of fast-growing plants, such as squash and melons. At planting time, it's easy to peel away the paper without damaging the roots.

ON HAND: Used yogurt containers

TURN THEM INTO: Seed-starting pots

HOW TO DO IT: Simply wash them out, poke a few small holes in the bottom, add seed-starting mix, and plant!

ON HAND: Opaque plastic sweater boxes

TURN THEM INTO: Mini greenhouses for seed starting

HOW TO DO IT: Put small seed trays filled with sterile potting soil and your seeds inside these boxes, water from below, close the lid and set the boxes in a warm place until the seeds germinate. Then put the opened box under a set of fluorescent shop lights and watch the seeds grow.

LET THERE BE LIGHT

Cuttings, germinating seeds, and indoor plants all benefit from direct light—something easily accomplished with an overhead lighting system. Here's how Lynn MacMahon of Flushing, New York, builds hers.

"I use a shop rack system and turn the steel shelving upside down, which makes a tray with a lip around it," MacMahon explains. "Then I line the shelf with heavy plastic and fill it with cat litter or perlite. I cover the shelf with nylon window screening and set the pots on top of the screening. The screening keeps the pots from sinking in and the cat litter keeps the environment humid. I hang shop lights for the bottom shelf from the shelf above and hang shop lights for the top shelf from the basement rafters." You could try this same setup in a garden shed or garage, as long as you have a source of electricity.

GOING TO GREAT LENGTHS

All the seed packets give planting directions such as, "plant 2 to 3 inches apart," "plant in hills 2 to 3 feet apart," "plant 6 inches deep," and so on. But, how many gardeners do you know who carry yardsticks?

Use a permanent marker to mark off inches on your trowel, or inches and feet on the handle of your shovel or hoe. You can even mark off gallons on the inside of your bucket. Knowing how long your shovel is will also help you calculate heights of walls and trees and distances between objects. Even better, measure your body parts and memorize the lengths of your fingers, arms, reach, and height. You may forget your yardstick, but chances are good you won't go to the garden without your fingers!

and one in the middle of each long side of the flat. Cover the bottom of the tray with cat litter or perlite, and then put the pots in the tray.

Next, loop a piece of electrical wire from each corner hole to the opposite corner hole, and twist the ends in place to secure. Likewise, loop a piece through the two middle holes, and twist to secure. Finally, put a clear plastic bag over the entire setup, and tuck the bag under the tray or close it with a twist-tie. The electrical wire frame will keep the plastic up off of the seedlings.

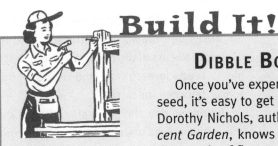

Build It!

DIBBLE BOARD FOR SEED TRAYS

Once you've experienced the fun of growing plants from seed, it's easy to get carried away with indoor seed sowing. Dorothy Nichols, author of *Tips and Secrets for a Magnificent Garden*, knows all about that: Each year, she raises thousands of flower, herb, and ornamental grass seedlings for her Moscow, Idaho, all-organic, demonstration garden. To help speed up her sowings, she constructed a "dibble board" to create the proper size seed holes for her particular seed starter—an 8 × 12-inch Perma-Nest plant tray. You can make your own to fit your favorite seed-starting flat. Here's how:

Materials

Scrap piece of ¼-inch outdoor plywood

¾-inch galvanized roofing nails

Saw

Ruler or yardstick

Drill with ³⁄₃₂-inch bit

Hammer

DIRECTIONS

1. Measure your existing seed-starting flat and cut the plywood slightly smaller to fit just inside.

2. With the pencil and ruler or yardstick, draw lines 1½ inches apart across the plywood, lengthwise and widthwise. (This ensures that your dibble board will produce evenly spaced holes in the flat.) Drill a ³⁄₃₂-inch pilot hole at each point where the lines intersect.

3. Drive the nails through the holes, all the way to the heads.

DIBBLE BOARD

SEED-STARTING FLAT

GADGET GOLD MINES

Do you have a sponge brush and hors d'oeuvre picks at home? Then you have some instant garden gadgets. Here's how you can use these items for your seed-starting efforts.

Hors d'oeuvre picks are handy for thinning out seedlings, suggests Chaz Macdonald of Center Valley, Pennsylvania.

Sponge paintbrushes with wooden handles are perfect for disinfecting the corners of six-pack pots, reports Macdonald.

ON HAND: Plastic, under-the-bed storage box

TURN IT INTO: Potting soil mixing bin

HOW TO DO IT: Put the box on your potting bench, tool bench, or kitchen table. Scoop in the ingredients of your potting medium (soil, peat moss, compost, and the like), mix it all together, and fill your pots. When you're finished, leave any leftovers inside, snap on the lid and tuck the box under your bench—or under your bed—till you're ready to pot up more plants.

GOOD NIGHT, COZY SEEDLINGS

Dyed-in-the-wool gardeners like to squeeze out as much growing season as they can. To do just that, Marina Wojciechowski of Lansdale, Pennsylvania, combines a raised bed cold-frame with bricks to cheat the cold weather. Wojciechowski fills the frame with leftover bricks—the kind with three holes in them—spacing the bricks 2 inches apart. She pushes the bricks into the soil until the soil level is flush with the top of the bricks. Wojciechowski plants seeds in each hole and in the 2-inch spaces between the bricks.

During the day, the sun warms the bricks, which retain some of that heat during the cold overnights. Wojciechowski's brick trick helps her get an early jump on spring, starting zinnias and other semihardy plants this way. In about 2 weeks, or when the seedlings are abut 2 inches high, Marina gently lifts the bricks and pushes the seedlings out of their holes for transplanting or hardening-off. The seedlings in the 2-inch-wide spacer strips are easy to just lift up once the bricks have been removed.

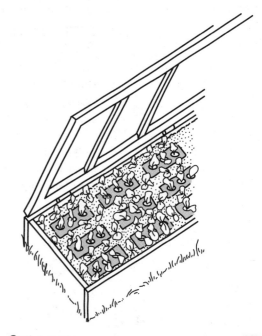

GET A JUMP ON SPRING BY LINING A COLDFRAME WITH SCAVENGED THREE-HOLE BRICKS. THE BRICKS WARM UP QUICKLY AND MAKE PERFECT SEED "FLATS."

Storage Savers and Tool Organizers

Say good-bye to the days of lost garden gadgets. With a bit of brainstorming, storage will be a breeze and your seed, note, and tool-hunting days will be over. In this section, learn how to make your own "String Thing," "Plant Condo," seed recipe box, and tool caddy.

FILE UNDER "SALADS"?

Keep your seed packets organized with the help of a recipe box. Label the dividers according to type of seed (annuals, perennials, greens, vegetables, and so on), and stash the seed packets there. For seed you've collected at home, put the seed in one of those tiny self-sealing plastic bags you can purchase at a jeweler, and label it with a permanent marker.

SEEDS ON ICE

Andrea Ray Chandler, ace garden writer and photographer from Olathe, Kansas, stores all her seed packets in tight-sealing Tupperware containers. Before she shuts and "burps" the lid, she tosses in any desiccant packets that she finds in new shoe boxes. The boxes then go into her spare fridge, where the seeds will remain viable for several years.

SAFE FOR ALL YOUR FINE HERBS

Don't have room to hang your herbs to dry? Susan Albert, Texas author of the acclaimed China Bayles herbal mysteries, has found that the best way to dry her herb harvest is to use a portable sweater dryer. This simple device, available at many department stores, has a 2-foot-square mesh screen that's supported by 8-inch, foldable legs. Pick your herbs in the morning after the dew has dried off, then place them flat on the rack in the shade on a dry day. The rack works especially well for small-leaved herbs, such as thyme.

PLANT CONDO

After remodeling her kitchen, Anne Cunningham, a writer for the Bay Area Gardener Web site, found herself with a number of white, plastic-coated wire storage baskets. The gardening lightbulb went off in her mind, and she envisioned these baskets as the perfect shelves for her numerous seedlings and transplants. Because these baskets stack, she could place the plants that require lots of sun on the top shelf and those that need shade underneath. The whole structure is very compact and looks quite colorful against the side of her house. Snails and slugs have trouble getting through the wire, but water gets through easily. If you can't find old wire baskets, you can buy new ones in all shapes and sizes at most home centers and hardware stores.

WELL NOTED

If you have trouble keeping track of your gardening notes and packets of leftover seeds, try using the binder system that Vermont garden writer Warren Schultz cooked up. Schultz admits he isn't the most organized gardener but says that his binder system is foolproof. To follow his example, you'll need a three-ring binder, four-pocket plastic photo sleeves, index cards, and a pen.

Schultz earmarks an index card for every pack of seeds, and after he sows the seeds, he writes all the relevant information on that card. When he's finished, he seals the seed pack with a piece of tape, then puts the pack and its index card into the same pocket of a photo sleeve. He inserts the sleeve into the binder and stores the binder on a shelf in a cool, not-too-sunny location.

Schultz takes the binder out into the garden with him to make notes on the cards, and then easily slips them back into the correct pockets. If he needs to make a second or third sowing of any variety, he knows right where to find the seeds. At the end of the gardening season, he slips a packet of silica gel or other desiccant into one of the pockets and stores the whole binder in a cool, dry place until the following year.

STRING THING

Gardeners go through a lot of string for tying, trellising, and marking out rows and beds. Those in the know realize that the large cones

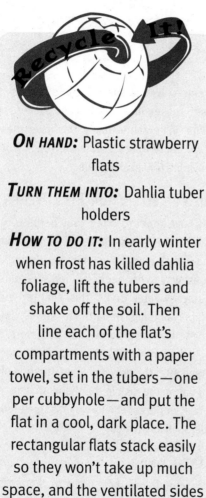

ON HAND: Plastic strawberry flats

TURN THEM INTO: Dahlia tuber holders

HOW TO DO IT: In early winter when frost has killed dahlia foliage, lift the tubers and shake off the soil. Then line each of the flat's compartments with a paper towel, set in the tubers—one per cubbyhole—and put the flat in a cool, dark place. The rectangular flats stack easily so they won't take up much space, and the ventilated sides will keep needed air circulating to the tubers all winter long.

of cotton garden string are very cost-effective. But if you've ever tried to use one, you also realize that it's bulky and hard to handle and keep clean in the garden. What's more, you've probably longed for a third hand to help out—or at least a better way of managing the cone. Well, here's one! Using just a bleach bottle, Cheryl Coston of Fairdealing, Missouri, built her own "string thing," which makes dealing with these large cones easy.

To make a string thing, cut a flap in the side of a bleach bottle, making it large enough to slip the cone in. Then poke a hole in the cap with an ice pick. Set the cone inside the bottle and thread the end of the string through the cap. Stick a couple of pieces of Velcro on the flap so you can open and close it. Carry the string thing by the handle, and pull out the string as needed through the cap. All the while, the string stays clean and dry inside.

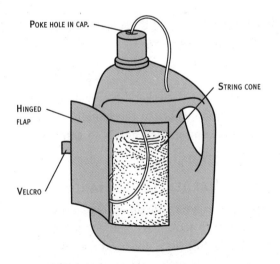

POKE HOLE IN CAP.

STRING CONE

HINGED FLAP

VELCRO

WITH A FEW SIMPLE MODIFICATIONS, A BLEACH BOTTLE MAKES A HANDY CADDY FOR CARRYING STRING WHEREVER YOU NEED IT IN THE GARDEN.

Recycle It!

ON HAND: Old filing cabinet

TURN IT INTO: Tool storage chest

HOW TO DO IT: An old metal or wooden file cabinet makes a great place to store hand tools, pruning tools, string, gloves, and all kinds of miscellaneous garden items.

A SPICY IDEA FOR SEED STORAGE

Viewing a herbarium at a seed laboratory gave Linda Harris, a Master Gardener from Fulton, Kentucky, a nifty idea for saving her own flower seeds from year to year. She uses an old wooden spice rack and recycled glass spice jars or pill bottles. The rack has three shelves and can hold about 15 bottles.

Linda collects seeds from faded garden flowers and lets them dry thoroughly. Then she pours the seeds into a clean, dry bottle and caps it. She says she also keeps leftover flower seeds from store-bought packets this way. (It's also good for herb seeds and small- to medium-size vegetable seeds.) "The bottles keep everything organized neatly and protect the seeds from humidity in the air," Linda says. "I use adhesive tape to label the bottles and write the flower name and

Build It!

RUST-AND-DIRT-DEFYING TOOL BAG

"I never used my fancy tool bags because I didn't want to get them dirty," says Carolyn Roof of Paducah, Kentucky. "Most hand-tool bags are heavy-duty canvas or lined with plastic. A wet tool left in the bag can easily rust, especially in our humid climate. The answer to wet tools and dirty bags came in the form of landscape fabric. You can buy it at any garden center; it comes in a roll about 45 inches wide, and it is available in various thicknesses. Choose the thickest fabric available for this project. It is soft, lets moisture out, is black, and is washable. Finally, I have a tool bag I really use."

Materials

½ yard of 45-inch-wide landscaping fabric

Scissors

Sewing machine and thread

DIRECTIONS

1. Lay fabric out flat on cutting surface. Cut two 3-inch-wide strips from the short side for handles.

2. Fold each 18 by 3-inch strip in thirds lengthwise, to make it three layers thick. Stitch along the center of each handle, sewing all three layers together.

---

date on the tape with a ball-point pen." Her seed rack hangs on a hook in her mudroom, where the air is cool most of the time, and there's no direct sunlight. Once she's slipped on her gardening, the seeds are right there at her fingertips.

A PEACHY CARRYALL

If you enjoy buying peaches or other fruit direct from local orchards, you may have some extra peach baskets around your house or garage. Don't let them gather dust in a corner. They're a great lightweight carryall for the garden. Toss some hand tools into a basket for easy transport to the garden, or use it for collecting garden debris to carry to the compost pile.

KEEP GARDEN TOOLS HANDY

Tired of running to the garage every time you need a tool? Save yourself some steps by trying this great idea: Attach a standard mailbox to a post right in your garden and use it to store some of your most-used hand tools and gloves. If you're like most gardeners, every time you walk through the

3. Fold down 1 inch on each short side of the remaining fabric. Stitch the fold in place to create the top hem.

4. Stitch one handle to each hemmed edge of the bag, placing the ends of the handle about 6 inches in from each outer edge of the fabric. To secure the handles, stitch in a square and then reinforce it by stitching an X over the squares.

5. Fold the body in half with the top seam folds to the outside. Sew up each side, allowing ½-inch seam allowance (creating the bag). Stitch again ¼ inch from your first row of stitching to reinforce the seam.

6. Turn bag right side out, stuff with tools, and go.

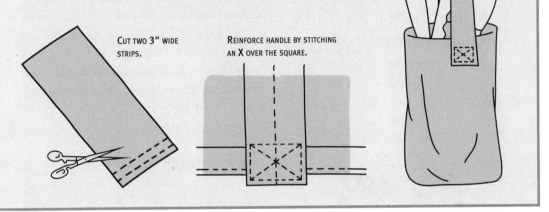

CUT TWO 3" WIDE STRIPS.

REINFORCE HANDLE BY STITCHING AN X OVER THE SQUARE.

FILL WITH TOOLS AND YOU'RE READY TO GO.

yard, you find weeds to dig, spent flowers to snip, or branches to trim. Once you have a garden mailbox, your garden gloves, trowel, and pruners are handy whenever you need them!

A BUCKET CARRYALL

Old drywall-compound pails are free for the taking wherever you find drywallers and painters working. Warren Schultz of Essex Junction, Vermont, salvaged one and turned it into a garden carryall. Here's how to make your own: Wash and dry the bucket. Heat the end of a screwdriver over a fire or with a blow torch, and melt holes just below the lip of the bucket, spaced every 4 inches. Tie a nail apron (available from a hardware store) around the lip of the bucket with the pockets on the outside. Poke holes through the fabric to correspond to the holes in the bucket. Lace a leather shoelace through the holes to fasten the apron to the bucket. Put your seeds, notepaper, and pencils in the pockets and your hand tools in the bucket, and you have a handy way to carry all your gardening stuff wherever you need it!

ON HAND: A fishing vest

TURN IT INTO: A convenient place to store labels, marking pens, tissues, and seeds

HOW TO DO IT: Nothing to it. Just put on the fishing vest, pack the pockets, and head out to the garden.

ON HAND: A carpenter's belt

TURN IT INTO: A tool caddy

HOW TO DO IT: Strap on the belt, insert your tools, such as a trowel and pruners, and you're all set.

MOWER CADDY

"When mowing, I always seemed to find a twig that needed cutting, but it didn't get cut because the pruners were hanging in the house. The pruners just won't stay in my pocket," says Carolyn Roof of Paducah, Kentucky. "I came up with a simple solution. A carpenter's cloth apron is a wonderful hand-tool carrier that you can wear for either riding or push mowing."

She recommends making this modification to hold the tools in place in the apron: Cut a piece of 1-inch-wide elastic so it's slightly longer than the width of the apron pocket. Pin the elastic along the top edge of the pocket, stretching to fit. Anchor stitch at each end, and then sew the elastic to the apron at several points. You can wear the apron, or tie it on the mower seat back or the handles of the push mower. Add pruners, a sharpener, a pruning saw, and a water bottle, and go. Your tools will stay securely in the elastic-snugged pocket.

THE GARDENER'S "BRIEFCASE"

You can use a nail apron tied around the outside of a 5-gallon plastic bucket for holding seeds, pruners, and tools. Fill the bucket with larger tools or garden supplies when going to and from the garden. Attach the lid to the bucket with a duct-tape hinge to create a waterproof supply trunk, or seat. Commercial garden tool buckets include inner, stacking trays, but resealable plastic bags work fine for thrifty gardeners.

DRY SOAK

You really can recycle anything. Case in point: Turn that old foot soaker into a tool or weed caddy. Bring it along to the garden and put

Build It!

OLD-TIME TOOL CADDY

If you want the look of a weathered oldie without the antique-shop price tag, do what Juneau, Alaska, gardener Natasha Zahn Pristas did: Build your own. Here's how she did it.

Materials

Two 1-inch-thick boards for ends, each 9 × 7¼ inches

Finish nails

Three 1-inch-thick boards for bottom and sides, each 19½ × 7½ inches

1½-inch-diameter dowel, about 19 inches long

Paint or stain (optional)

Saw

Drill

Hammer

DIRECTIONS

1. Cut the two rectangular end pieces so their sides angle to a top width of 3½ inches, as shown in the illustration below.

2. Predrill the nail holes, and nail the bottom and side panels together.

3. Predrill nail holes for the angled end pieces, and nail them to the sides and bottom of the box.

4. Measure the dowel for a tight fit, and cut it to the inside length of the box (it will be roughly 18½ inches). Predrill nail holes in ends of caddy. Make pilot holes in dowel.

5. Nail the dowel/handle in place.

6. Paint or stain the box, or leave it to weather naturally.

9" × 7¼" BOARD

DOWEL

19½" × 7½" BOARD

Build It!

CONTAINER CORRAL

If you garden in containers on a roof deck or wind-swept terrace, or—as Victoria Hawley does in Portland, Oregon—on a houseboat, this bottomless frame could save your prized plants from taking to the sky in a stiff breeze.

Materials

You can use whatever lengths of materials suit your needs. This size is designed to use five office-sized plastic garbage cans for containers.

Four 6½-foot 1 × 2s

Eight 10-inch 1 × 2s

Screws or galvanized nails

Eight 16-inch 1 × 2s

¼-inch plywood to form the front, back, and sides

Three 4-foot 1 × 2s (optional)

One 7-foot 1 × 2 for crosspiece (optional)

Paint, stain, or varnish (optional)

Screwdriver or hammer

DIRECTIONS

1. Screw or nail two 6½-foot 1 × 2s and two 10-inch 1 × 2s together to form a rectangle. Screw or nail two 10-inch 1 × 2s 27 inches in from each end to form a reinforcement large enough for the center container (this will be the bottom part of the frame). Make a second rectangle the same way (this will be the top part of the frame).

2. Screw or nail one of each of the 16-inch 1 × 2s to a corner of the bottom frame, including the center rectangle, so that the 1 × 2s are vertical.

3. Attach the top frame to the tops of the vertical 1 × 2s.

4. Screw or nail a piece of plywood facing to each side of the frame; overlap front of facing over sides of facing.

5. For the optional trellis, nail three 4-foot-long 1 × 2s vertically to one long side of the frame. Nail the 7-foot-long 1 × 2 horizontally across the vertical 1 × 2s, a few inches from their tops.

6. Paint or stain the finished product as desired and set in your containers. Leave the bottom open for drainage. Place the pots on 1 × 2 scraps for drainage.

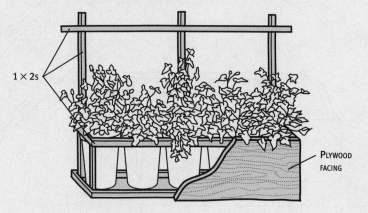

1 × 2s

PLYWOOD FACING

weeds in it as you pull them out, or fill it with tools before you head out to the garden so you can carry everything you need at once.

A Tisket, a Tasket

A totable basket! Made from three used coffee cans, this nifty flower-collecting tote is the ultimate in recycling. Linda Harris of Fulton, Kentucky, says that she finds it's best to use coffee cans of the same size to keep the tote balanced. It's also a nice touch to spray paint the cans to add an artistic touch.

After the paint is dry, set the first can on a level surface. Wrap and tie one end of a ball of twine around the can. Wrap the twine around the can several times, then wrap it around a second can, pulling the second can close to the first one. Wrap the twine around the second can several times, then repeat the wrapping for a third can. The cans will form a triangle. Wrap the twine all the way around the outside of the three joined cans until the cans are tightly lashed together. Knot the twine securely in the wrapping on one side.

To make a comfy twine handle, cut three lengths (or six for a wider handle) of twine about 36 inches long. Holding the twine

lengths together as if they were one, knot them to the twine on one side of the can tote. Braid or twist the lengths, then knot them to the twine on the opposite side of the tote.

Keep flower cutters or hand pruners in one of the cans, and fill the two other cans with water to take to the garden when cutting flowers. The water-filled cans will keep your cut flowers fresh and wilt-free until you get back to the house to arrange them.

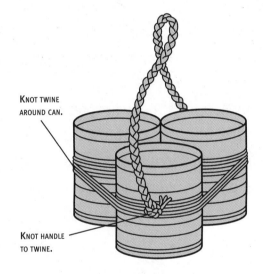

KNOT TWINE AROUND CAN.

KNOT HANDLE TO TWINE.

TIE METAL COFFEE CANS TOGETHER FOR A HANDY CUT-FLOWER TOTE.

Trellises and Supports

Running out of room in your garden? Think "up"! Use bicycle wheels, chopsticks, baby gates, and tomato cages to make trellises, arbors, and other supports that will spread your plants upward instead of outward. Read the following tips to find out more about creating plant supports and how to best use them in your garden.

GORGEOUS GARAGES

The front of most garages are pretty stark, but they don't have to be that way. You can dress up your garage door with perennial twining vines— good choices are kiwis (*Actinidia* spp.), five-leaved akebia (*Akebia quinata*), Dutchman's pipes (*Aristolochia* spp.), bittersweets (*Celastrus* spp.), sweet autumn clematis (*Clematis terniflora*), jasmine, and pyracanthas. Other vines are suitable also, as long as they won't grow taller than 20 to 30 feet.

On either side of the garage door plant your vine of choice (just be sure it won't grow taller than 20 to 30 feet). Install galvanized eye screws in regularly spaced intervals up the sides of the door and above the door. (Do this so you can thread the wire in a zigzag pattern.) For larger vines, install the screws all the way up to the roof. Then thread galvanized wire through each eye, looping it around the eye screws at least once—and, voilà, you have a sturdy wire trellis, and within a year or two, that baked stretch of garage front will be a sea of greenery. (Give the vines a good pruning two or three times a year to keep them in check.)

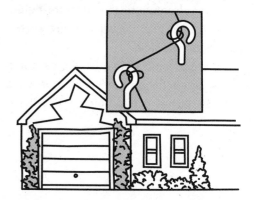

USE AN ON-THE-WALL VINE TRELLIS TO TURN A DULL GARAGE FRONT INTO A SEA OF GREEN.

CHICKEN OUT YOUR VINES

Each time a heavy wind whips up, Tucson, Arizona, gardener Sue Giles can expect to see some of the mature vines that cloak her neighbor's adobe house flopping in the yard. That's because twining-type vines don't cling well to adobe without a trellis, and many homeowners don't want to install supports, fearing they'll damage the adobe. But Giles came up with a novel solution to the problem at her own home. She nailed chicken wire to unseen portions of her roof, allowing the vines to secure themselves to the wire.

This method works best if you have a flat roof where you can install the chicken wire out of sight. But small amounts of chicken wire could be nailed to angled roofs, too, especially if the wire is spray painted first in a color that matches the roof.

FISHING FOR A TRELLIS

Clear monofilament fishing line makes one of the fastest, lowest-maintenance, and most invisible trellises there is. Simply hammer in a pattern of nails into your house where you want vines to grow, adding a dab of paint to conceal the nails. Then twist and tie on the fishing line.

CREATE AN INVISIBLE TRELLIS IN MINUTES USING FISHING LINE.

WINE AND ROSES

Part of the fun of gardening is finding new uses for unusual items. Martha Neal always keeps her eyes peeled for interesting objects to complement her many beds and borders on her 10 acres in Hamden, Connecticut. When she spotted several nifty copper-colored promotional wine racks in her local liquor store, she knew right away how lovely her morning glories would look twining up the curved metal sides. After a few well-placed "bribes" of cookies and coffee to the store staff, they gave the racks to her when the promotion was over. Neal set the 6-foot-high, freestanding racks in her gardens and weighted the bases down with some of the ever-present rocks from her New England soil. All her vining annuals and perennials enjoy the spirited supports, and Neal enjoys the classy look they lend to her winter landscape.

CAGED BEAUTIES

Few garden sights are as sad as beautiful peony blooms sprawling face down in the mud. But if you've ever priced those commercial peony hoops, you're likely looking for a less expensive staking solution. Jan Hale Barbo, the garden columnist for the *Santa Fe New Mexican,* has the answer!

After planting 50 peonies around her Espanola, New Mexico, home, Barbo tried using those inexpensive, cone-shaped, 3-foot-high tomato cages that are sold at most hardware stores. However, once the cages were installed, she noted that "the bare metal looked horrible and shiny and detracted from the graceful beauty of my peonies." Barbo solved this problem by grouping all the cages together in the back of an old trailer and spraying them with hunter green paint. Now she has perfect flower supports:

ON HAND: Siberian iris leaves

TURN THEM INTO: Organic twine

HOW TO DO IT: Use Siberian iris leaves instead of garden twine or plastic wire twist-ties for tying up tomato bushes, staking lilies, or any taller veggie or perennial. This material is very durable, says Minnesota gardener Don Engebretson, and it turns a pleasant golden brown, giving your garden a kind of country look.

"They blend and disappear into the landscape even before the foliage emerges enough to hide them." She also finds that these colored cages work great for other tall and floppy flowers such as Oriental poppies (*Papaver orientale*).

UNDERWIRE SUPPORT

Those plant supports you see in the catalogs are neat, but they're also expensive. So why not build your own? That's what Master Gardener Bob Mortiz of Sioux City, Iowa, does. He bends a 72-inch length of #9 galvanized wire into a circle, leaving about 30 inches on one end ver-

tical. Then he sticks the straight end of the wire into the soil—and, voilà, an instant plant support. Mortiz notes that this support works great by itself, or you can make a bunch of supports and place them in a circle, which he says works wonders holding up peonies in bloom.

SAVE MONEY BY MAKING YOUR OWN PLANT SUPPORTS OUT OF WIRE.

SAFE AND STRETCHY PLANT TIE

When it's time to trellis her vegetable plants, Cheryl Coston of Fairdealing, Missouri, raids the clothes drawer. "I use old T-shirts and socks cut into strips as plant ties," she says. "They're very strong and stretchy, so they give as the plant grows. Dark colors, except red, blend in with the foliage and aren't noticeable after a week or so, when the color fades."

WINDOW FRAME TRELLIS

Nothing conveys the romance of a cottage garden quite as well as a window surrounded by clematis, roses, or other flowering vines. Caroline Jumper of San Jose, California, has developed a very simple and inexpensive way to get that look. Using a few simple materials, she and her husband have constructed removable supports for vining flowers all around their house (and along a fence as well).

All it takes is some 12- to 14-gauge wire, four 2- to 3-inch-long eye screws, and a turnbuckle for each window trellis. Install the eye screws into the side of the house at the corners of the window (or wherever desired). Run a length of wire through all four eye screws, then attach the free ends to the turnbuckle (position this wherever you can reach it easily). "The eye screws keep the wire a few inches from the house, which is enough room for good air circulation," Jumper says. "And the turnbuckle allows us to tighten the wire as needed or remove it easily when it's time to paint or take the roses down for serious pruning."

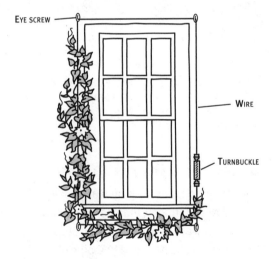

EYE SCREW

WIRE

TURNBUCKLE

GIVE YOUR HOME A COTTAGE-GARDEN LOOK BY CREATING WINDOW TRELLISES FOR FLOWERING VINES.

REBAR TO THE RESCUE

Climbing roses and flowering vines add a touch of country charm to any garden. To show off his climbers, Bill Robinson of Sierra Madre, California, prefers arbors and teepee-shaped sup-

ON HAND: Old tent frame parts
TURN THEM INTO: Garden trellis
HOW TO DO IT: Put together the tent frame or frames—without the tent—then place in a sunny location in your garden. Cut pieces of heavy string long enough to reach your plants. Tie one end of each string to the top of the frame and gently wrap the free end around the stem of tomatoes, peas, or other vines to guide them upward.

port structures, but he found that commercial trellises were quite expensive. So he decided to make his own, and he found the perfect material to make them: concrete reinforcing metal, or rebar. "You can buy a 20-foot length of $\frac{1}{4}$-inch rebar at a home-supply store for a couple of bucks," Robinson says. "It's very strong but relatively easy to work with, and it turns a lovely shade of rust after being exposed to the elements, which blends in with the stems."

To make a rebar teepee, take a 20-foot length of $\frac{1}{4}$-inch rebar, grab it firmly by one end, and enlist a friend to do the same at the other end. Place the center point of the bar against a strong post, then walk toward each other until the rebar is bent into a U. Repeat with a second piece of rebar. Carry the bent rebar to the garden and push the ends of one U into the ground as far as you can. Prop a length of 2 × 4 against it if needed to hold it upright while you get the second piece in position. Place the second U over the first, oriented in the opposite direction to create a cross pattern at the top. Push the second U into the ground until the arches meet at the top center, then fasten them together with wire. "I train all kinds of climbers to grow up and through this simple structure, and it looks lovely," Robinson says.

To make a rebar arbor, bend two 20-foot pieces of rebar as you would for a teepee, but don't make the bend so sharp: You want the ends to be 5 to 6 feet apart. Push the ends of the first length of arch into the ground enough to stabilize it. Place the second arch parallel to the first arch, 1 to 2 feet away, and push the ends into the ground. Cut five or six crosspieces of rebar to length with a hacksaw—they should overlap the arches a couple inches on each end. Fasten the crosspieces to the arches by wrapping wire in an X pattern around each intersection.

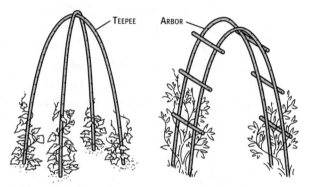

TEEPEE   ARBOR

REBAR MAKES A GREAT MATERIAL FOR A VARIETY OF VINE SUPPORTS. BOTH TWINING AND TENDRIL-CLIMBING VINES FIND IT EASY TO GRAB. IT'S LOVELY WITH ROSES, TOO!

DOZENS OF USES FOR PLASTIC PIPE

"Plastic pipe is fun to play with," says Sally Roth of New Harmony, Indiana, who enjoys devising new ways to use the cheap, durable material. So far, she has used PVC pipe to fashion trellises, make columns to hold butterfly feeders and birdbaths, to support floppy plants, and to predator-proof her birdhouse posts. "I never work from a pattern or plan," she says. "I just figure it out as I go along. I've only had two problems with it so far: First of all, that white pipe sticks out like a sore thumb, so I paint it a dark color that blends in better. (See "Build It!" on page 125 for de-

ON HAND: Old Christmas tree

TURN IT INTO: Pole bean trellis

HOW TO DO IT: "Replant" the old tree by sinking it into a hole deep enough to keep it upright. Then plant your pole beans around the bottom but away from the trunk a bit so they get enough light.

Build It!

BICYCLE-WHEEL TRELLIS

Frank Fowlie, a Master Gardener from Mountain View, California, turned an old bicycle wheel into a unique trellis for his runner beans and erected it in a raised bed. Here's how to do it.

Materials

1 metal pipe, slightly smaller in diameter than the hole in the wheel

Three lag bolts

28-inch bicycle wheel

Nails or tent pegs

Twine

Drill

Hammer

DIRECTIONS

1. Drill three holes 1 inch down from the top of the pipe, and insert the bolts so they stick out about an 1 inch to support the wheel.

2. Pound the pipe into the ground and set the wheel in place over the pipe.

3. Hammer a nail into the edge of the raised bed directly under each spoke. If you don't have a raised bed, you can use tent pegs pounded directly into the soil.

4. Attach one end of a piece of twine to each nail, run the twine up over the spoke above the nail, and back down again, and attach this end of twine to the nail. Repeat this process for each nail.

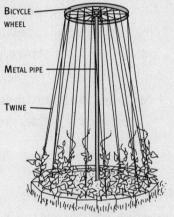

BICYCLE WHEEL

METAL PIPE

TWINE

tails.) Second, raffia and wire slip off the pipe, so when I want to make trellises, I use duct tape to fasten the ends, then wrap with raffia to hide the tape."

HELP YOUNG VINES CLIMB

To help tiny vining plants—such as sweet peas, morning glories, and thunbergias—find their way to a trellis, tie string around the head of a long nail. Sink the nail into the ground next to the seedling and tie the string onto the trellis. Attach the vine (gently!) to the string with a twist-tie.

GIVE SMALL VINING PLANTS A SENSE OF DIRECTION BY GUIDING THEM TOWARD THE TRELLIS.

ON HAND: A wooden clothes-drying rack

TURN IT INTO: A trellis

HOW TO DO IT: Simply unfold the rack in the garden and push the legs into the soil to secure it in position. Sow or plant creeping plants beneath the rack. Use twist-ties to secure their vines to the rack as they grow.

BABY GATES GROW UP

Inexpensive, versatile, and storable: Those are the qualities that most of us look for in trellises. Becky Turner of Bowling Green, Indiana, found the perfect material when she viewed a common object from a different perspective. Now she haunts garage sales for used baby gates, and turns them into instant trellises in her garden.

For sprawling crops that don't climb too tall, such as cucumbers, Turner simply stretches a gate out, pushes the bottom 1 or 2 inches into the dirt, and anchors it with 5- to 6-inch-long garden staples. (For extra stability, hammer two 1 × 2 posts into the ground at each end of the gate and attach them with cord, wire, or reinforced packing tape.) As your crops grow, help their vines climb over the support. For climbing plants like morning glories, Turner stands a gate on end beside a wall or post and anchors the bottom to the ground with garden staples. She then expands the gate and, using heavy-duty twist-ties, fastens the other end with screws or nails driven into the wall or post.

Don't have a baby gate available for trellising? The sturdy metal springs from an old crib make a good substitute! For a freestanding trellis, sink two 5-foot-tall, 2 × 2 posts about 1 foot deep into the soil and as far apart as the width of the springs. Stand the springs on end between the posts, and lash the springs securely to the posts using wire or rope. To use the springs against a wall or fence, screw four eye screws into the wall or fence, conforming to the dimensions of the spring frame, and fasten the springs to it using wire or rope. Sow or set climbing plants at the base.

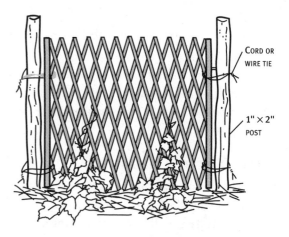

JUST BECAUSE YOUR KIDS ARE GROWN DOESN'T MEAN YOU HAVE TO THROW OUT THAT BABY GATE; TRANSFORM IT INTO A GARDEN TRELLIS.

Build It!

STEEL CABLE SPOOL TRELLIS

Spent steel cable spools are commonly free for the hauling and offer tempting design possibilities despite their rough appearance. With a little ingenuity, you can create a beautiful trellis that you won't need to hide in the back lot. (If you can't find an abandoned spool by the side of the road, call your local telephone or cable TV company.)

Materials

Empty wooden steel cable spool

Three 1½-inch wood screws

6- to 8-foot-long wood pole (1½-inch dowel or hand-rail stock)

2-inch galvanized roofing nails

Big ball of heavy-duty string

Seeds

Screwdriver

Hammer

Ax or saw

DIRECTIONS

1. Prepare a level site for the trellis by clearing an area about 3 feet wider than the actual spool. Position the spool so it's stable—use wood shims to level if necessary.

2. Insert the three 1½-inch screws at even intervals around the pole about 1 inch below the top end. Place the other end of the pole through the middle of the spool and hammer it into the ground until it is secure—about 1 foot deep is good. (Use an ax or a saw to shape a point on the end of pole if the soil is hard.)

3. Hammer galvanized roofing nails spaced 3 inches apart around the base and top of spool, leaving ½ inch of the nail head exposed.

4. Tie strong string securely to a nail at the base of the spool. Run the string up to the top of the spool and twist it around a nail once or twice, and then run the string to the top of the pole and twist it around a screw. Then run the string down to the base of the spool and begin again. Repeat the process until all the nails are strung and the trellis is complete. If you run out of string, simply tie a new piece of string to the nail and begin threading the string again.

5. Plant seeds or transplants around the base of the trellis. If needed, train young vines to the string by securing them with twist-ties. Before long, that old spool will be hidden behind a glorious display!

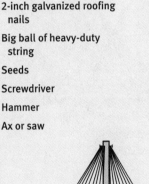

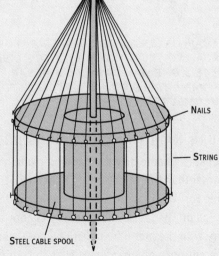

NAILS

STRING

STEEL CABLE SPOOL

Rebar the King

One of the great quests for gardeners, especially vegetable gardeners, is the search for the perfect staking material. Linda Monier of Olive Branch, Mississippi, believes she's found the right stuff: concrete reinforcing metal, commonly known as rebar.

"I thought of it when we were building a new garage next to our house and had to go buy rebar for the foundation," says Linda. Admiring the 20-foot-long metal rods for their strength and durability, she realized they would make perfect, indestructible trellises. But first, the rebar had to be cut down to size. "I just had my husband, Marty, buy a few extra 4-gauge rods, the thickest diameter, and cut them into thirds with an acetylene torch." Marty suggests you could instead cut them with a hacksaw, or have the concrete supply house cut them to your specifications. "I use them for staking tomatoes, beans, or whatever needs it," Linda says.

That's not all. "We also cut some in half and used them to create an A-frame with plastic netting on both sides for my cucumbers. The fruits grow straighter and longer, and I have a great place to get out of the summer sun in the garden! I can also plant my summer lettuces under the A-frame to keep the intense heat off of them."

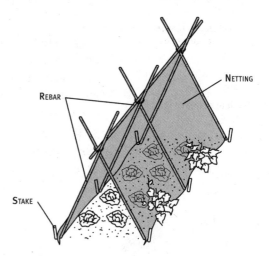

REBAR MAKES A GREAT MATERIAL FOR CREATING STURDY, DURABLE TRELLISES. HERE'S ONE WAY TO BUILD A REBAR A-FRAME TRELLIS THAT'S PERFECT FOR CUCUMBERS.

Turn Rain Gear into Sunshine

Not sure what to do with that ripped umbrella? Rather than throw it away, try Bea Kline's trick. This Fort Washington, Pennsylvania, gardener strips off the fabric and creates a canopy topiary with the metal frame. Try two of these at the entrance of a garden or even in your vegetable bed for a striking, formal look.

Recycle It!

ON HAND: Old chopsticks

TURN THEM INTO: Houseplant supports

HOW TO DO IT: Dig those old chopsticks out of your kitchen drawer and put them to good use as a support for tall, floppy, or twining houseplants.

Living Garden Art

Create a sure conversation piece with a worn-out lawn chair! Simply remove the tattered webbing from a metal lawn chair, and secure the chair frame to the ground with U-shaped metal pins over the bottom bars. According to Bea Kline, of Fort Washington, Pennsylvania, you can create an interesting, large-scale topiary. A fast-climbing vegetable like scarlet runner beans is all you need. Plant seeds or transplants around the base of the chair—and, voilà, your "living" chair will be a definite ice breaker for your next garden party.

Build It!

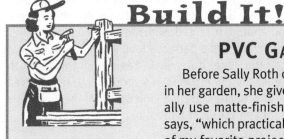

PVC Garden Entry Posts

Before Sally Roth of New Harmony, Indiana, uses any PVC in her garden, she gives it a quick spritz of spray paint. "I usually use matte-finish black or very dark green-black," she says, "which practically disappears among the greenery. One of my favorite projects was a pair of simple PVC gateposts that defined the entrance to a hot-colored butterfly garden of orange, yellow, and red flowers. I sprayed those pipes bright cobalt blue. It made me feel as if I were in Mexico."

Materials

Spray paint in your choice of color

Two 7-foot sections of 5- to 6-inch-diameter PVC pipe

Two PVC end caps, to fit pipe, and glue

Gallon bucket of ordinary soil (for each pipe)

Level

Funnel

Shovel or post-hole digger

Directions

1. Spray paint pipes and caps. If coverage is spotty, let dry and apply a second coat of spray paint.

2. Dig a 2-foot-deep hole for each post, using a shovel or post-hole digger. Have a helper hold the pipe in place while you backfill. Use a level to keep the posts plumb. Tamp thoroughly with feet. While the helper supports the pipes, pour a bucket of soil into each, using the funnel to weight the bottom ends.

3. Attach end caps to one end of each pipe section with glue, as per supplier's instructions. Let dry. Touch up with spray paint if needed.

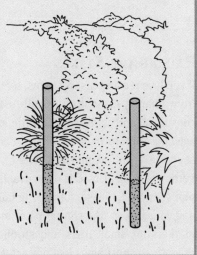

Build It!

TWIG TRELLIS

"When I moved to a new home where the electric meter was situated in an extremely unattractive place on the house wall facing the swimming pool, I built a decorative twig trellis to hide it," says Barbara Reese Yager of Charlotte, North Carolina. She collected branches until she had enough for the design, and then used supplies she had on hand to complete it. "The result was a perfectly lovely focal point against the wall, which also cleverly screened the meter from view." Yager built this trellis to fit a specific wall space. You can adjust the dimensions of your trellis to fit any area you like by selecting longer or shorter branches. Train a vine on the trellis (clematis would be very attractive in a sunny location) or just let it stand decoratively.

Materials

4 attractive tree branches, 8 to 10 feet long and 1 to 1½ inches in diameter

6 to 8 attractive tree or shrub branches, 5 to 6 feet long and ½ to 1 inch in diameter

Baling twine or rawhide strips

Mounting nails or mortar pins (depending on the surface to which you're attaching it)

Pruners

DIRECTIONS

1. Collect the branches. If you have woods on your property, you can gather them there. If not, call a local tree-trimming service to see if they can provide what you need.

RAISING THE STAKES

If you love reusing cast-off items, try these tips from Charles Cresson, horticulturist, garden consultant, and author from Swarthmore, Pennsylvania. Broom handles, mop handles, and such make sturdy, nicely finished stakes for garden use. He also adds old galvanized water pipes (no lead, please) for staking taller plants and young trees. The shorter pipes make good markers for small trees and shrubs. Simply drive three short pipes in a protective triangle around the young plant. The pipes protect from trampling and mower damage, he notes. Cresson also likes concrete rebar for tall perennials and young trees. "The natural color blends well with the landscape, rebar lasts forever, and it never breaks as other stakes often do with time," he says. "If you don't have any lying around from that last foundation or driveway project, many home centers sell short lengths or will cut long pieces to any length you need," Cresson remarks.

2. Lay the four longer branches (the uprights) on a flat surface such as a floor or patio, spacing them about 12 inches apart. Use the larger-diameter ends as the bottom, lining them up so the base will be even.

3. Lay the smaller branches (the crosspieces) across the uprights in a pleasing pattern. They can be spaced equidistantly, as shown here, or placed against the uprights in any pattern you like. Leaving a stub, start lashing a crosspiece to an upright, wrapping twine in an X. Several wraps for each side of the X should be sufficient. Cut and fasten off the twine.

4. Repeat for each joining, until every joint is lashed and fastened.

5. Using pruners, shape and finish off the ends of the uprights and the stubs of the crosspieces so they are eye-pleasing to you.

6. Lash the finished trellis to nails, mortar pins, or fence posts.

7. Plant a vine at base, if desired.

LASH A CROSSPIECE TO AN UPRIGHT BRANCH BY WRAPPING TWINE IN AN X.

FUN FENCE-POST FINIALS

"I wanted a pretty finishing touch for the handmade wooden fence my neighbor crafted for me, but didn't want to spend a fortune on fancy carved finials," says Caroline Whitenack of Doylestown, Pennsylvania. "So I got the idea to use 4-inch clay flower pots to top the fence posts."

Whitenack painted the pots to match the fence, using outdoor latex paint. If your pots fit snugly over the fence post, there's no need to secure them further. If the pots wiggle and slide off the fence posts, Whitenack has an ingenious trick for keeping them in their place: For each fence post, cut a short piece of 1/4-inch wooden dowel the same height as each pot, and then drill a 1/4-inch-diameter × 3/4-inch-deep hole in the top of each fence post. Glue the dowel in place. When the glue dries, set the pots upside down over the top end of the fence posts. Whitenack said that the pots looked so cute that she received many compliments. And the pots wintered well outdoors to boot!

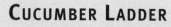

Build It!

UNDRESSED UMBRELLA

So a recent windstorm de-frocked your patio umbrella? Don't throw it out. Instead, turn it into a topiary frame. Here's how. Sink a section of PVC pipe into the ground and pop in the umbrella shank. (If your umbrella has a curved handle, you may have to cut that off first with a saw.) Plant ivy at the base, and train it up the shaft and then later out across the spokes.

SODA POP SIX-PACK TRELLIS

Here's a creative way to get a second use out of plastic six-pack holders: Turn them into a trellis. All you need besides the holders are some twist-ties and either dowels or 2 × 4s. Simply fasten the six-hole plastic rectangles together with twist-ties to make a trellis of any size and shape you want. Thread dowels through the top and bottom rows of holes and fasten the top dowel to a wall or hang it between 2 × 4s sunk into the ground. Portland, Oregon, gardener Susan LeMaster says, "It's perfect for annual vines like peas. At the end of the summer you stash it away for next year." If you decide to dispose of it instead, check to see whether your local recycling center will accept it. If you must throw it in the trash, cut all the rings apart first so they won't be a hazard to wildlife."

STAKE YOUR CLAIM

When it comes to plant staking, Chela Kleiber, director of education at Tyler Arboretum near Media, Pennsylvania, takes full advantage of recycling. She scours her property for well-forked fallen branches, then uses them to support asters in an unobtrusive way. "It's a very British practice," she says, "and a nice, natural look." These won't work for large heavy plants like hollyhocks, but for midsize clumps like asters they're great, like a cupping hand. Besides fallen branches, you can save prunings, too, for this naturalistic—and free—way to stake floppy plants.

Build It!

PORTABLE BAMBOO ARBOR

When you want shade and privacy in a hurry without the expense, bother, and long-term commitment of a construction project, try this fast alternative from Marianne Lipanovich, who gardens in Redwood City, California. It costs a pittance, goes together fast, and—best of all if you're a gardener on the go—you can pack it up in a snap and move it to another area of your garden.

Adjust the size and the number of support rails to suit your space and the weight of the vines the arbor will support. Lipanovich designed hers to be 12 × 6 × 8 feet. Single crosspieces on three sides provide stability and growing space for lightweight vines.

DIRECTIONS

1. Set four 8-foot bamboo poles into the pots, and anchor the poles with sand and stones. Pour potting soil on top of the sand and stones to further steady the poles.

2. Fasten two 12-foot bamboo poles and two 6-foot bamboo poles to the tops of the upright poles with nylon cord or rope, using the lashing technique shown in the illustration below.

3. Add two more 12-foot poles and two more 6-foot poles as supports midway up the upright poles using the same lashing technique.

4. Sow seeds or set plants into the pots.

5. Tie twine or nylon netting to the top and sides if your vines need added support.

Materials

Four 8-foot bamboo poles, 1½ inches in diameter

Four sturdy terra-cotta pots, 18 to 20 inches in diameter

Sand and stones

Potting soil

Four 12-foot bamboo poles, 1½ inches in diameter

Four 6-foot bamboo poles, 1½ inches in diameter

Nylon cord or rope

Seeds or plants

Twine or nylon netting, if desired

Utility knife or scissors

USE THIS LASHING TECHNIQUE FOR POLES.

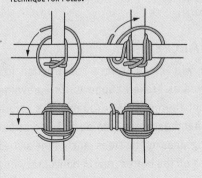

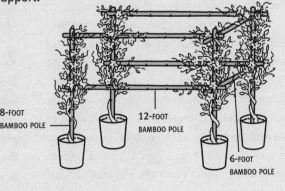

8-FOOT BAMBOO POLE

12-FOOT BAMBOO POLE

6-FOOT BAMBOO POLE

ON HAND: Willow and alder prunings

TURN THEM INTO: Unobtrusive plant supports

HOW TO DO IT: Simply bend them into arches and push the ends into the soil around plants that tend to flop.

ROMANTIC WOVEN BRANCHES

Mimi Hoag of San Leandro, California, uses twigs and branches for many garden projects. "I use long, slender twigs (such as forsythia and willow) to make hoop supports for perennial plants and pea vines. The twigs blend in so well, the supports are completely unnoticeable. Sometimes they even take root! Honeysuckle vines are great for weaving into baskets, with or without other materials."

There's also every gardener's favorite project—the twig fence. Insert strong, shorter branches vertically into the ground along the line where you want the fence for the posts. (They can be of any height.) Then take longer, slender, flexible branches (with or without leaves) and weave them into the vertical branches in patterns. "You'll have a unique garden accent that everyone will rave about," assures Hoag.

SELF-CENTERING TREE STAKES

Generally, young trees don't need staking, but if your site is windy or has loose, sandy soil or if the tree is particularly top heavy, you may need to stake it for the first growing season. But excessive or uneven pressure on a young tree trunk is just as bad as no support at all. Bungie cords take all the trouble and guesswork out of the job. Simply drive the stakes equidistant from the tree trunk. Then wrap one or more bungie cords around each stake and the tree and hook their ends together. Use the same number and size cords on each side. For best results, remove stakes once the tree is strong enough to support itself.

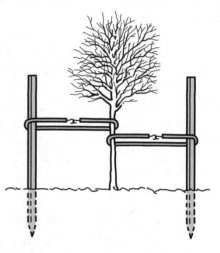

A COUPLE OF STAKES AND BUNGIE CORDS PROVIDE EXCELLENT SUPPORT FOR YOUNG TREES.

WIRE ARCHES

Leftover wire mesh from a construction job works well as arched supports for sprawling vines. Cut the mesh into roughly 3 × 5-foot pieces, bend each one into an arch, and train the young vines up the sides. Anchor the arches by cutting off the bottom row of horizontal wires and sinking the vertical wires into the ground.

Build It!

PLASTIC, FANTASTIC TRELLIS

Ed Bender of Carlsbad, California, wanted to grow peas, beans, and flowering vines along a 5-foot-high white fence that surrounds his backyard. "And I wanted a trellis that would be both portable and good-looking," he says. Bender realized that PVC pipe would make perfect trellis material. "It's more durable than wood, and less noticeable against the white fence." And he soon found out that building a trellis from PVC was an easy job.

Materials

Two ½-inch PVC elbows

Clear PVC glue

½-inch-diameter, schedule 40 PVC pipe cut into the following lengths:

   3 sections cut to 5 feet

   4 sections cut to 3 feet

   2 sections cut to 3 inches

Four ½-inch PVC Ts

1-inch-diameter PVC pipe cut into two 6-inch lengths

Two #6 hooks

1-inch-gauge chicken wire or nylon netting

DIRECTIONS

1. Working on a solid, flat surface, glue a PVC elbow to the top of two of the 5-foot lengths of PVC.

2. Glue a PVC T to the top of the remaining 5-foot length.

3. Making sure that they're square and level, glue a 3-foot length of PVC into each of the horizontal openings of the T.

4. Glue the other end of the 3-foot lengths into the elbows to form an M-shape frame as shown.

5. Glue a T to the bottom of the center 5-foot length, as shown.

6. Glue a T to the bottom of each of the outside 5-foot lengths as shown, and glue a 6-inch length of PVC into the bottom of those two Ts.

7. Glue the remaining 3-foot lengths into the horizontal openings of the Ts.

8. Stand the trellis up against the fence, and mark the ground where the feet hit.

9. Sink the two lengths of 1-inch PVC into the ground, at those marks against the fence.

10. Screw two hooks horizontally into the fence about 3 feet apart with the open end of the hooks oriented up.

11. Hang the top part of the trellis on the hooks and slide the trellis legs into the PVC anchors.

12. Fasten chicken wire or nylon netting over the frame to complete the trellis.

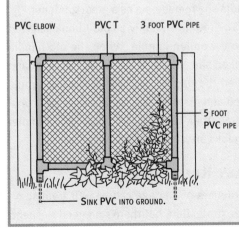

PVC ELBOW   PVC T   3 FOOT PVC PIPE

5 FOOT PVC PIPE

SINK PVC INTO GROUND.

Weed
Control

Weeds are one curse that afflicts the lowly gardener. One day the weeds are gone, the next, they're back. But weeding doesn't have to feel like a bad case of the plague. With the right weeding tools and preventive techniques, the road to weed-free living is fairly smooth. Read on to find out how to " 'Hoe' Happy as a Clam."

"HOE" HAPPY AS A CLAM

Whether you live near the seashore or not, a short-handled clam rake can be the perfect thing for cultivating and freshening a garden bed. The rake's slender tines penetrate the ground deeply, bringing up rhizomes of grasses and other invasive weeds in large pieces that are easy to pick out of the soil. Market gardener George DeVault lives and farms in Pennsylvania, but he swears by his clam rake. "It's a lot less work than chopping away at weeds or hardened soil with a hoe," DeVault says.

If you don't live near the seashore, you may wonder where to buy a clam rake. One option is to order a clam rake especially designed for gardeners by Real. (See "Resources" on page 144 for ordering information.)

WEEDER EXTRAORDINAIRE

Uncle Paul's J-hook weeder is Pennsylvania gardener Melanie DeVault's favorite homemade tool. "It was great for getting in under my climbing rosebushes and hosta and even shrubs to clear out the scraggly weeds without bending over, or sticking a hand in and fearing encountering a garden snake or something," DeVault says with a laugh. DeVault inherited the original J-hook weeder from her Uncle Paul, whom she remembers as a great gardener.

The tool was simply an old J-hook screwed into a wooden handle. When the old handle broke, she was heartbroken. Her husband saved the day by heading out to the supply shed and fashioning a replacement by screwing another large J-hook into a hoe handle. (J-hooks are cheap at hardware stores.)

EASY KNEELING PAD

Gardeners of any age can benefit from some knee protection, but there's no need to spend money on a fancy commercial kneeling pad.

Barth Getto, a longtime gardener who lives outside of St. Louis, Missouri, suggests checking with your local carpet store for old carpet samples. Getto happens to be in the carpet business himself, so he has ready access to 36 × 16-inch carpet samples, and he says they make great pads for kneeling in the garden. "I often double the samples up in the early spring to keep my knees warm and dry," he says. For a really cushy experience, "I scrounge up a piece of foam and sandwich that between two carpet samples. These pads are best-sellers at our neighborhood garage sales!"

SUPER HOE I

Faced with weeding his 1½-acre pumpkin patch, Steve Hammerstone of Easton, Pennsylvania, took a look at his hoe and knew he needed a more comfortable and durable implement. "Why not make myself a tool that not only holds up to heavy hoeing but also fits my body better?" mused Hammerstone, a metal sculptor and market gardener. When he next visited his hardware store, he spotted an inexpensive ice chopper and knew he could convert it into his own personalized weeding machine.

Hammerstone put the head of the ice-chopper into a strong vice with the handle pointing straight up. He carefully heated the neck with a propane torch until it was not quite red hot, and then bent the handle down to form an almost 90-degree angle. (To be safe, be sure to wear eye protection and heavy leather gloves while using the torch.) After the tool cooled, he painted the metal to prevent rusting. Hammerstone now has a custom hoe with a head heavy enough to

chop up the toughest weeds and a handle long enough to let him stand up straight while doing so.

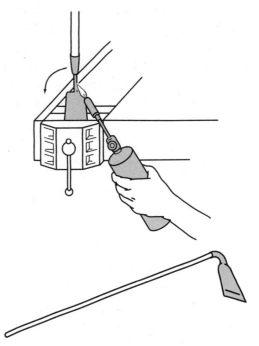

IT'S EASY TO CONVERT AN INEXPENSIVE ICE CHOPPER INTO A STURDY, LONG-HANDLED HOE. JUST HEAT THE NECK OF THE CHOPPER TO SOFTEN THE METAL, THEN BEND DOWN THE HANDLE!

SUPER HOE II

Champion recycler and Philadelphia gardener Will Anderson grew up across the street from a large vegetable plot tended by an older Italian gentleman. This sturdy gardener walked for miles to come hand-tend his garden, and he always arrived shouldering an equally sturdy handmade tool that he used to break, lift, and cultivate the heavy clay soil. When Anderson and his dad expressed interest in his Old World creation, the old man pantomimed how he heated the tang of a large flat-tined garden fork, bent it at a right angle, and then mounted it onto a longer, straight shovel handle. He wielded the tool by swinging it down from overhead and using the long handle to lever up the skewered earth. Anderson and his dad made their own version and used it to great effect in their own garden. It especially works well for pulling up sod, but "you better watch your toes!" adds Anderson.

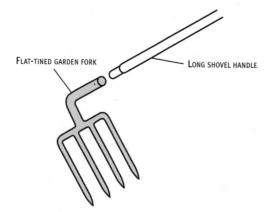

FLAT-TINED GARDEN FORK — LONG SHOVEL HANDLE

TAKE TWO TRADITIONAL TOOLS—A FORK AND A SHOVEL—AND PUT THEM TOGETHER, AND YOU HAVE A SUPER NEW TOOL THAT'S GREAT FOR A VARIETY OF GARDEN TASKS!

TREE RAKE

Living in Bertram, Texas, means living with bindweed. It grows everywhere—even up into the trees! Bill Albert, noted author of the Robin Paige Victorian mysteries, found that a potato rake is the finest bindweed removal tool in the business. This cross between a hoe and a pitchfork has three very sharp tines that easily snare the bindweed and bring it down for disposal. This rake is also useful for dragging piles of thorny clippings or for pulling compost out of a bin.

BASIC BLACK FOR HERBS

Gardeners everywhere know that black plastic is great for suppressing weeds, warming the soil, and conserving water. But don't think its use is limited to just the vegetable garden! Jim Weaver, a market gardener in Bowers, Pennsylvania, finds this material is perfect for his cut-your-own herb beds. "I've had fantastic success with sages, thymes, lavenders, and especially basils, which love the extra heat. I've even overwintered common rosemary!" he exclaims.

Weaver lays the plastic mulch down in the spring, punches holes in it, and plants the herbs in a staggered double row. As the closely spaced plants grow, their leafy canopies prevent the soil from getting too hot. The shade also protects the plastic, so Weaver can reuse the same sheets for up to three seasons. Another bonus? Weaver rarely has to water his rows of herbs. They grow all by themselves, ready for his customers to harvest their favorites.

NEVER-DIE DENIMS

The knees may be shot, or they may no longer fit, but you just can't kill an old pair of denim blue jeans, says Joan Janssen, editor of *Sage Leaves*, the newsletter of the Wisconsin unit of the Herb Society of America. She transforms her old jeans into durable kneeling pads. She cuts the leg portions into 12- to 14-inch lengths and stuffs them with rubber carpet pads, old soft sponges, bed pads, or even folded copies of the *Wall Street Journal*. Then she folds the edges and secures them with duct tape, string, or clothespins.

If you cut a longer piece, you can simply tuck the ends inside without fastening. Or, if you're feeling domestic, stitch the ends closed with a large needle and heavy thread, and add a denim loop to hang or carry them about. The jean-pads last for years, are recycled, free, and easy to clean (just unstuff and throw in the washer).

WEED ISOLATORS

If you find weeds poking up through your groundcovers, don't fret about how to dig them out. Here's a trick for dealing with the problem quickly and effectively without digging. First, cut the bottom one-third or one-half off a 1- or 2-liter plastic soda bottle. Then gather the weed's leaves into the bottle bottom, place the spray nozzle of an organic herbicide such as Weed-aside into the neck, and give the weed a blast. The bottle concentrates the deadly spray onto the weed and spares the groundcover from any damage.

DON'T LET ORGANIC HERBICIDES DRIFT ONTO DESIRABLE PLANTS! KEEP THEIR SPRAY WHERE YOU WANT IT BY ISOLATING WEEDS WITH A SODA-BOTTLE SHIELD.

Recycle It!

ON HAND: Old straight or Phillips-head screwdriver whose tip has become dented or mangled

TURN IT INTO: Precision weeder

HOW TO DO IT: Just stick it in between pavers, flagstones, or cracks in your sidewalk and gouge out the weeds.

CURTAIN ROD WEEDER

Do sore muscles, a stiff back, or other aches and pains keep you from tending your garden? This simple tool may help. Thea Steinmetz, a Cleveland garden writer, recalls meeting an elderly, severely handicapped gardener who had made a nifty weeder from an old curtain rod (the two-piece rectangular type that expands). With a tin snips, she cut a V-notch in the end of the straight length of one piece. (The shorter bent section makes a perfect built-in handle.) She would wait until after a rainfall when the ground was wet, and then push the notched end into the earth right next to a weed. With a slight twist of the wrist, the weed would pop right out!

Build It!

EASY KNEELER

Aging joints won't stop 87-year-old Harvey DiGiorgio of Pittsburgh from tending his heirloom tomatoes and peppers. "At my age, the hardest part is getting down to the soil and then back up again." DiGiorgio's solution was to build a simple kneeler with side grips to steady him when getting up and down in the garden. The pipes that form the bottom help to keep the kneeler stable and prevent it from getting stuck in the mud. Below are the directions for reproducing DiGiorgio's kneeler, but feel free to experiment with the size to make the kneeler most comfortable for you. Be sure to use $3/4$-inch PVC, not $1/2$ inch, which would be too weak.

Materials

$3/4$-inch PVC pipe, cut with hacksaw as follows:

    Two 20-inch pieces

    Four 12-inch pieces

    Four 8-inch pieces

    Four 2-inch pieces

Eight $3/4$-inch L-fittings

Four $3/4$-inch T-fittings

PVC primer and cement

$1/2$-inch exterior plywood (about 18×24 inches)

Four $1/4 \times 1 1/2$-inch carriage bolts and nuts

Old carpet or foam padding, heavy plastic, or sturdy cloth (optional)

Staple gun and staples (optional)

Drill with $1/4$-inch drill bit

Nail or awl (optional)

Handsaw

DIRECTIONS

1. Fit the PVC pipe pieces together, as shown in the diagram. Don't use the adhesive at this point; you just want to make sure all the parts fit together.

2. When you're ready to permanently assemble your kneeler, start with the rectangular base first, gluing each joint together one at a time. Follow the instructions that came with the PVC cement. (Typically, you prime each part of the joint first, apply the glue, and then squeeze the parts together.) Make sure the four T-fittings are all pointing directly upward, perpendicular to the base.

3. Glue together the parts that form the upright supports.

4. Drill four ¼-inch holes into the long pipes of the base, near the corners (see diagram). It may help to start the holes by nicking the surface of the pipe with a nail or awl.

5. Cut the plywood to fit the kneeler frame. Position the plywood on the frame and mark the location of the mounting holes. Drill the four holes with the ¼-inch bit. Attach the plywood with the carriage bolts and nuts.

6. To make the kneeler easy on your knees, use a loose piece of old carpet or foam padding on top of the plywood. To make the padding a permanent part of the kneeler, cover the foam with heavy plastic or sturdy cloth secured to the underside of the plywood with staples.

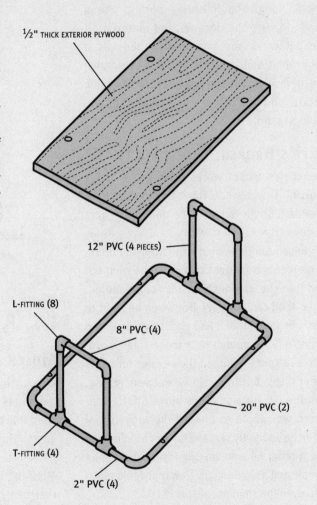

½" THICK EXTERIOR PLYWOOD

12" PVC (4 PIECES)

L-FITTING (8)

8" PVC (4)

20" PVC (2)

T-FITTING (4)

2" PVC (4)

Double-Duty Mulch for Pathways

Here's a way to have your mulch and sheet compost too! In spring, cover garden pathways with newspaper or cardboard. Spread straw, grass clippings, weeds, and other biodegradable material over the newspaper to hold it in place. Enjoy weed-free paths all season long. The following spring, use a spade to slice the decomposed material off the pathways and into garden beds as a convenient source of rich humus. Re-mulch the pathways with newspaper and organic debris, and you're off and growing for another season.

If It's Broken, Don't Fix It

Sometimes a tool works even better if it's broken! That's what Tony Nelson-Smith of Swansea, South Wales, in the United Kingdom discovered.

Nelson-Smith needed a tool to help him remove weeds from tight spaces, so he went out and bought an inexpensive, long-handled, three-toed claw weeder. But when he went to work, he found that it had about two claws too many; it just wouldn't fit in those small, hard-to-reach spots. He used the weeder for some other tasks, but the weld wasn't very strong, and the two outside claws broke off. Nelson-Smith was about to discard the broken tool when he suddenly realized he was holding just the weeder he was looking for! It had a long handle and a single sharp claw that could reach into even the smallest of spaces.

"Now I use it for hoeing in very constricted spaces (like between rows of seedlings in a nursery bed), for clearing between rocks or paving slabs, and for uprooting individual weeds," Nelson-Smith says. "It does jobs for which most other tools are too clumsy. I regard it as quite essential."

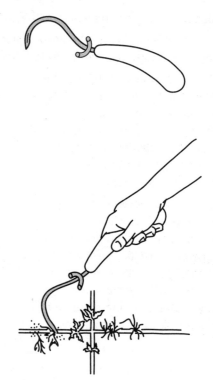

WHEN THIS THREE-CLAWED WEEDER LOST TWO OF ITS CLAWS, IT BECAME AN EVEN MORE VALUABLE TOOL.

Mulch Magic

When using plastic mulch or landscape fabric, gardeners face the eternal problem of how to keep it in place easily, inexpensively, and elegantly. Sure, you can use those ready-made garden staples, but Mike Coston of Fairdealing, Missouri, invented a new and improved staple that beats the store-bought ones in several ways. Coston's stakes cover more ground, cost next to nothing in materials, and are so easy to make that he can put together two or three of them per minute.

Build It!

WEED SCRAPER

If you grow corn, you know how important weed control is for getting a good harvest. Kris Lopez Fitzgerald and Shawn Fitzgerald of Stillwater, Oklahoma, raise native varieties for seed for a local seed conservancy, so they spend a lot of time caring for their corn crop, and they just weren't satisfied by conventional hoes and hand weeders. Unless used very carefully, the broad blades endangered the small sprouting corn plants. With a little ingenuity, Shawn came up with a perfect corn-weeding tool. It worked so well, it even earned a name: the "Weed Scraper!"

Materials

Wooden broom or mop handle

Brass strip, 1/16 inch × 3/4 inch × 10 inches

1/8-inch bolt and nut

Stainless steel lashing cable

Hacksaw

Drill with 1/8-inch steel bit

DIRECTIONS

1. Cut the wooden handle to a 12-inch length with the hacksaw.

2. Again using the hacksaw, cut a 1-inch-deep notch across the center of the flat end of the handle.

3. With a 1/8-inch drill bit, drill a hole through the end of the handle, perpendicular to the notch, 1/2 inch from the end.

4. Bend the brass strip into a flattened loop, bringing the two ends together to form a tab.

5. Insert the tab into the notch, and mark drill holes on the tab through the holes in the handle.

6. Remove the tab and drill holes at the mark with the drill bit.

7. Reinsert the tab into the notch, slip a bolt through the holes, and secure it with a nut.

8. Wrap the lashing cable around the notched end of the handle to hold the tab in place and prevent the blade from wiggling.

Kris says the Weed Scraper works especially well on young weed and grass seedlings, and it's most effective when the soil is moist but not soggy. "Our corn seedlings were already up when I weeded with the tool, and I found I had great control in tight places using it."

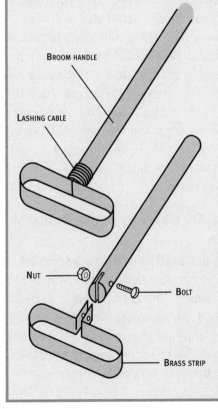

BROOM HANDLE

LASHING CABLE

NUT

BOLT

BRASS STRIP

ON HAND: Newspaper and shredded paper

TURN IT INTO: Mulch, compost, and plant protection

HOW TO DO IT: Use newspaper as a mulch by laying four to six sheets down over garden paths. Scatter grass clippings over the newspaper to make it a little more attractive. Shredded household mail, bills, and other paper can also be added to your compost pile, says Irv Breber of Bensalem, Pennsylvania.

Caroline Whitenack of Doylestown, Pennsylvania, uses sheets of newspaper as plant protection when nights get chilly. She places a flat upside down over her plants, and then covers it with a few sheets of newspaper until morning.

To make the staples, start with a coil of 12-gauge galvanized wire (similar to that used for coat hangers). Cut the wire into 21-inch lengths. Using pliers, bend about 7 inches on each end downward to form two legs. Then, bend the middle down about 1 inch so that the wire forms a capital M. That leaves a 7- to 8-inch-wide staple. Because these are so much wider than store-bought staples, you won't need very many. "For a 4 × 16-foot bed, I use one at each corner and two or three down each long side," Coston says.

Do you prefer to hold plastic mulch or landscape fabric in place by burying the edges in the soil? Traditional wisdom advises digging a trench around the mulched area, tucking in the edges, and backfilling with soil. That's a lot of work, but Coston's wife, Cheryl, has a much better way. She uses an old lawn edger with a dull blade to tuck in the mulch. Here's how: "Just lay out the plastic or landscape fabric over the area you want to cover, allowing some slack. Place the edger on the mulch material about 6 inches in from the edge, and then put your foot on the edger and push down. The edger will pull out, leaving the fabric securely in soil," Cheryl explains.

DRIVE OUT WEEDS FROM BRICK PATHS

Getting out dandelions, chickweed, and other pesky weeds from between the patio bricks was a frequent chore, says organic gardener and plant photographer Rick Mark of Vancouver, Washington, because hand-pulling commonly broke off the tops of the plants, leaving the roots, which quickly regrew.

"I tried a trowel and a dandelion digger," says Mark, "but they were too big to fit between the bricks," which were laid in a sandy base atop gravel and soil. "So I dug out the longest, strongest flat-head screwdriver I could find. Its shaft was just the size I needed to slip between the bricks and pry out dandelions and other deep-rooted weeds."

The screwdriver makes quick work of less tenacious weeds and weed seedlings, too, says Mark. "I can drag it down a row between the bricks in less than a minute, and uproot everything in its path." When he's done getting out the weeds, he shakes off the soil, piles the weeds for compost, and sweeps loose soil and sand back into the cracks.

POISON IVY BARRIER

Carolyn Roof of Paducah, Kentucky, advises, "If you need an impervious barrier between you and poison ivy, try this: Put a plastic newspaper sleeve bag over your hand and arm like a glove before pulling out that piece of poison ivy. After you've pulled it out, peel the 'glove' inside out while you're still holding the weed. Then you can throw the whole thing away safely." There's no danger of spreading the plant oils as there is when you use garden gloves for the task. Bread bags work well for this, too. (You knew you were saving them for something!)

FORK IT OVER

A table fork is great for unearthing the roots of smaller weeds such as chickweed and knot weed. For bigger weed problems, try spreading roofing tar paper over the problem area for several weeks to smother weeds.

ON HAND: A mason's trowel

TURN IT INTO: A weeding tool

HOW TO DO IT: Put the trowel in a vise and bend the blade to a 90-degree angle. To use the trowel, stick the blade into the soil and pull the trowel toward yourself. "It does the job just as well as the expensive weeders in the garden catalogs, at about one-sixth of the price," says Jerry Anderson, a Master Gardener from Portland, Oregon.

A CARPET OF TOMATOES

Rolling out the carpet is exactly what home gardener Deborah Burdick of Mt. Vernon, Indiana, does when it's time to plant tomatoes. "When I wanted to expand my garden to make more room for tomatoes, my lawn care helpers suggested I try their technique: They unrolled an old piece of wall-to-wall carpet onto their lawn, cut holes in it, and planted their tomatoes in the holes. The carpet blocks

Build It!

MRS. BERRY'S FAVORITE WEEDER

The Berry Botanic Garden in Portland, Oregon, started its life as the cherished home turf of renowned plantswoman Rae Selling Berry. She designed and made a number of these weeders, several of which are still in use at the garden.

Materials

A sturdy branch or an old tool handle, about 6 inches long

2-foot piece of ¼-inch baling wire

Drill

Vise

Pliers

Metal file

DIRECTIONS

1. Drill a ¼-inch hole through each end of the branch or tool handle.

2. Put the baling wire into the vise, and bend the center portion into a D shape using the pliers.

3. Push the long ends of the wire through the holes in the handle, bending the tips tight against the end to fasten.

4. Bend the D-shaped opening to an angle of about 45 degrees.

5. With the file, sharpen the lower edge of the baling wire.

BRANCH OR OLD TOOL HANDLE

BALING WIRE

BEND TO A 45 DEGREE ANGLE

weeds, keeps the soil moist, and encourages earthworms."

Burdick finds carpet pieces at her local thrift shop, or begs them from friends, who are glad to oblige. She searches for natural-looking colors, such as browns and greens. After planting her patch, she covers the carpet with grass clippings all summer to hide the carpet. "You should see all the worms when I peel up a corner!" she exclaims. "No wonder my tomatoes do so well."

THROW IN THE TOWEL

"I love new, fluffy towels," says gardener Gretel Hartman of the Boston area. "I used to take the old thin ones to the thrift shop, until one day I realized they were all cotton—just another plant fiber that would gradually turn back to soil."

At first Hartman planned to tear the towels into strips and add them to her compost pile, but then she had an even better idea. "I had a roll of weed-blocking landscape fabric in my hand, ready to buy," she says, "when I remembered the towels. That's when I began using them as mulch around my shrubs and perennials. I lay them out as flat as possible, snipping here and there if I have to, and cover them with wood chips or grass clippings or compost, whatever beautifier mulch I happen to be using at the time."

Hartman says her old bath towels do an efficient job of smothering existing weeds and blocking new ones. And she noticed a bonus: "When Baltimore orioles came back in spring, they spied a piece of towel sticking out from the garden and went to work unraveling it for their nest."

Vegetable gardener Linda Howard of Evansville, Indiana, uses the same technique with old rag rugs that she scoops up at country auctions or thrift shops, or donates from her own house once they're past their prime. "They last 2 to 3 years," she notes, "and work better at blocking weeds and smothering grass than any other mulch I've tried."

Resources

To help you find great plants, garden supplies, and even more ingenious gardening ideas, we've compiled the following list of plant associations, gardening organizations, mail-order nurseries, garden suppliers, and product manufacturers. When you contact associations or specialty nurseries by mail, please enclose a self-addressed, stamped envelope with your inquiry. Notes in italics indicate particular products, plants, or services offered.

ASSOCIATIONS AND ORGANIZATIONS

American Dianthus Society
Rand B. Lee
P.O. Box 22232
Santa Fe, NM 87502-2232

American Horticultural Therapy Association
909 York Street
Denver, CO 80206-3799
Phone: (303) 331-3862
Web site: www.ahta.org

American Iris Society
Ada Godfrey
9 Bradford Street
Foxborough, MA 02035
Web site: www.irises.org

American Rose Society
P.O. Box 30000
Shreveport, LA 71130-0030
Phone: (318) 938-5402
Fax: (318) 938-5405
Web site: www.ars.org

Backyard Wildlife Habitat Program
National Wildlife Federation
8925 Leesburg Pike
Vienna, VA 22184-0001
Web site: www.nwf.org/habitats

Bio-Dynamic Farming and Gardening Association
Bldg. 1002B, Thoreau Center, The Presidio
P.O. Box 29135
San Francisco, CA 94129-0135
Phone: (888) 516-7797
Fax: (415) 561-7796
E-mail: biodynamic@aol.com
Web site: www.biodynamics.com

California Certified Organic Farmers
1115 Mission Street
Santa Cruz, CA 95060
Phone: (831) 423-2263
Fax: (831) 423-4528
E-mail: ccof@ccof.org
Web site: www.ccof.org

The Lady Bird Johnson Wildflower Center
4801 La Crosse Avenue
Austin, TX 78739-1702
Phone: (512) 292-4100
Fax: (512) 292-4627
E-mail: wildflower@wildflower.org
Web site: www.wildflower.org

The Maine Organic Farmers and Gardeners Association
P.O. Box 2176
Augusta, ME 04338
Phone: (207) 622-3118
Fax: (207) 622-3119
Web site: www.mofga.org

National Gardening Association
180 Flynn Avenue
Burlington, VT 05401
Phone: (802) 863-1308
Fax: (802) 863-5962
Web site: www.garden.org

North American Butterfly Association (NABA)
4 Delaware Road
Morristown, NJ 07960
Phone: (973) 285-0907
Fax: (973) 285-0936
E-mail: naba@naba.org
Web site: www.naba.org

North American Fruit Explorers (NAFEX)
1716 Apples Road
Chapin, IL 62628
Phone: (217) 245-7589
Fax: (217) 245-7844
E-mail: vorbeck@csj.net
Web site: www.nafex.org

Northeast Organic Farming Association (NOFA)
Web site: www.nofa.org
An affiliation of seven state chapters—CT, MA, NH, NJ, RI, VT. Check Web site for state contacts

Rodale Institute Experimental Farm
611 Siegfriedale Road
Kutztown, PA 19530
Phone: (610) 683-1400
Fax: (610) 683-8548
E-mail: info@rodaleinst.org
Web site: www.rodaleinstitute.org

Seed Savers Exchange
3076 N. Winn Road
Decorah, IA 52101
Phone: (319) 382-5990
Web site: www.seedsavers.org

Seeds of Diversity Canada
P.O. Box 36
Station Q
Toronto, Ontario M4T 2L7
Canada
Phone: (905) 623-0353
E-mail: sodc@interlog.com
Web site: www.seeds.ca

Wild Ones—Natural Land-scapers, Ltd.
P.O. Box 23576
Milwaukee, WI 23576
Web site: www.for-wild.org

BENEFICIAL INSECTS

Bountiful Gardens
18001 Shafer Ranch Road
Willits, CA 95490-9626
Phone: (707) 459-6410
Fax: (707) 459-1925
E-mail: bountiful@sonic.net
Web site:
    www.bountifulgardens.org

Gardens Alive!
5100 Schenley Place
Lawrenceburg, IN 47025
Phone: (812) 537-8651
Fax: (812) 537-5108
Web site: www.gardensalive.com

Gurney's Seed and Nursery Co.
110 Capital Street
Yankton, SD 57079
Phone: (605) 665-1671
Fax: (605) 665-9718
Web site: www.gurneys.com

Harmony Farm Supply and Nursery
P.O. Box 460
Graton, CA 95444
Phone: (707) 823-9125
Fax: (707) 823-1734
Web site: www.harmonyfarm.com

The Natural Gardening Co.
P.O. Box 750776
Petaluma, CA 94975-0776
Phone: (707) 766-9303
Fax: (707) 766-9747
Web site:
    www.naturalgardening.com

Peaceful Valley Farm Supply
P.O. Box 2209
Grass Valley, CA 95945
Phone: (530) 272-4769
Fax: (530) 272-4794
Web site: www.groworganic.com

Territorial Seed Co.
P.O. Box 157
Cottage Grove, OR 97424-0061
Phone: (541) 942-9547
Fax: (888) 657-3131
E-mail: tertrl@srv1.vsite.com
Web site:
    www.territorial-seed.com

BULBS

Breck's
6523 N. Galena Road
Peoria, IL 61632
Phone: (800) 804-6742
Web site: www.brecks.com

Brent and Becky's Bulbs
7463 Heath Trail
Gloucester, VA 23061
Phone: (804) 693-3966,
    (877) 661-2852
Fax: (804) 693-9436
E-mail:
    store@brentandbeckysbulbs.com
Web site:
    www.brentandbeckysbulbs.com

Bundles of Bulbs
PNB 349
1498 M Reisterstown Road
Baltimore, MD 21208
Phone: (215) 581-2188
Fax: (215) 862-3696

Dutch Gardens
P.O. Box 2105
Lakewood, NJ 08701
Phone: (800) 818-3861
Fax: (732) 780-7720
E-mail: info@dutchgardens.nl
Web site: www.dutchgardens.nl

McClure and Zimmerman
P.O. Box 368
108 W. Winnebago
Friesland, WI 53935-0368
Phone: (800) 883-6998
Fax: (800) 374-6120
E-mail: info@mzbulb.com
Web site: www.mzbulb.com

Van Bourgondien Bros.
P.O. Box 1000
Babylon, NY 11702-9004
Phone: (800) 622-9997
Fax: (800) 327-4268
E-mail: blooms@dutchbulbs.com
Web site: www.dutchbulbs.com

FLOWERS

Abundant Life Seed Foundation
P.O. Box 772
Port Townsend, WA 98368
Phone: (360) 385-5660
Fax: (360) 385-7455
E-mail: abundant@olypen.com
Web site:
    http://csf.Colorado.edu/
    perma/abundant

Kurt Bluemel, Inc.
2740 Greene Lane
Baldwin, MD 21013-9523
Phone: (800) 248-7584
Fax: (410) 557-9785
E-mail: kbi@bluemel.com
Web site: www.bluemel.com

Bluestone Perennials
7211 Middle Ridge Road
Madison, OH 44057
Phone: (800) 852-5243
Fax: (440) 428-7198
E-mail: bluestone@bluestone
    perennials.com
Web site:
    www.bluestoneperennials.com

Bountiful Gardens
18001 Shafer Ranch Road
Willits, CA 95490-9626
Phone: (707) 459-6410
Fax: (707) 459-1925
E-mail: bountiful@sonic.net
Web site:
    www.bountifulgardens.org

Burns Water Gardens
R.R. #2
Baltimore, Ontario K0K 1C0
Canada
Phone: (905) 372-2737
Fax: (905) 372-8625
E-mail: wtrgdn@eagle.ca
Web site: www.eagle.ca/~wtrgdn

W. Atlee Burpee and Co.
300 Park Avenue
Warminster, PA 18974
Phone: (800) 888-1447
Fax: (215) 674-4170
Web site: www.burpee.com

Busse Gardens
17160 245th Avenue
Big Lake, MN 55309
Phone: (800) 544-3192
Fax: (320) 286-6601
E-mail: customerservice@
    bussegardens.com
Web site: www.bussegardens.com

California Carnivores
7020 Trenton-Healdsburg Road
Forestville, CA 95436
Phone: (707) 838-1630
Fax: (707) 838-9899
E-mail: califcarn@aol.com
Web site:
    www.californiacarnivores.com
*Commercially propagated pitcher
plants* (Sarracenia *ssp.*)

Carroll Gardens
444 E. Main Street
Westminster, MD 21157
Phone: (800) 638-6334
Fax: (410) 857-4112
Web site: www.carrollgardens.com

Collector's Nursery
16804 N.E. 102nd Avenue
Battle Ground, WA 98604
Phone: (360) 574-3832
Fax: (360) 571-8540
E-mail:
    dianar@collectorsnursery.com
Web site:
    www.collectorsnursery.com

**Daydreamer Aquatic and
    Perennial Gardens**
225 Rumsey Road
Columbus, OH 43207
Phone: (614) 491-2978
E-mail: dowatdpg2@aol.com
Web site:
    www.daydreamergardens.com

Daylily Discounters
6212 W. SR 235
Alachua, FL 32615
Phone: (904) 462-1539
Fax: (904) 462-5111
E-mail:
    support@daylilydiscounters.com
Web site:
    www.daylilydiscounters.com

Ferry-Morse Seed Co.
P.O. Box 488
Fulton, KY 42041-0488
Phone: (800) 283-3400
Fax: (800) 283-2700
Web site: www.ferry-morse.com

Flowery Branch Seed Co.
P.O. Box 1330
Flowery Branch, GA 30542
Phone: (770) 536-8380
Fax: (770) 532-7825
E-mail:
    seedsman@mindspring.com
Web site: www.flowerybranch.com

Forestfarm
990 Tetherow Road
Williams, OR 97544-9599
Phone: (541) 846-7269
Fax: (541) 846-6963
E-mail: orders@forestfarm.com
Web site: www.forestfarm.com

Fragrant Farms, Inc.
413 Woods Lane
New Harmony, IN 47631
Phone: (888) 814-4665
Fax: (812) 682-4577
E-mail: mark@fragrantfarms.com
Web site: www.fragrantfarms.com

The Fragrant Path
P.O. Box 328
Fort Calhoun, NE 68023
*Seeds of fragrant, old-fashioned,
and rare plants*

Goodwin Creek Gardens
P.O. Box 83
Williams, OR 97544
Phone: (800) 846-7359
Fax: (541) 846-7357
E-mail: info@goodwincreek
    gardens.com
Web site: www.goodwincreek
    gardens.com

Greer Gardens
1280 Goodpasture Island Road
Eugene, OR 97401-1794
Phone: (541) 686-8266
Fax: (541) 686-0910
E-mail: orders@greegardens.com
Web site: www.greergardens.com

Heard Gardens Ltd.
5355 Merle Hay Road
Johnston, IA 50131
Phone: (515) 276-4533
Fax: (515) 276-8322
E-mail: info@heardgardens.com
Web site: www.heardgardens.com

Heronswood Nursery
7530 N.E. 288th Street
Kingston, WA 98346
Phone: (360) 297-4172
Fax: (360) 297-8321
E-mail: orders@heronswood.com
Web site: www.heronswood.com

J. L. Hudson, Seedsman
SR 2, Box 337
LaHonda, CA 94020

Jackson and Perkins
P.O. Box 1028
Medford, OR 97501
Phone: (800) 292-4769
Fax: (800) 242-0329
E-mail: service@jacksonand
    perkins.com
Web site: www.jacksonand
    perkins.com

Johnny's Selected Seeds
RR 1, Box 2580
Foss Hill Road
Albion, ME 04910-9731
Phone: (207) 437-9294
Fax: (207) 437-2759
E-mail:
    johnnys@johnnyseeds.com
Web site: www.johnnyseeds.com

J. W. Jung Seed Co.
335 S. High Street
Randolph, WI 53957-0001
Phone: (800) 297-3123
Fax: (800) 692-5864
E-mail: info@jungseed.com
Web site: www.jungseed.com

Logee's Greenhouses, Ltd.
141 North Street
Danielson, CT 06239-1939
Phone: (860) 774-8038;
    (888) 330-8038
Fax: (888) 774-9932
E-mail: logee-info@logees.com
Web site: www.logees.com

Dan Majeski Nurseries
P.O. Box 674
117 French Road
West Seneca, NY 14224-0674
Phone: (716) 825-6410
Fax: (716) 827-8537
E-mail:
    danjr@majeskinursery.com

Midwest Wildflowers
Box 64
Rockton, IL 61072
Phone: (815) 624-7040

Milaeger's Gardens
4838 Douglas Avenue
Racine, WI 53402-2498
Phone: (800) 669-1229
Fax: (262) 639-1855
E-mail: milaeger@execpc.com
Web site: www.milaegers.com

The Natural Garden
38W443 Highway 64
St. Charles, IL 60175
Phone: (630) 584-0150
Fax: (630) 584-0185

Niche Gardens
1111 Dawson Road
Chapel Hill, NC 27516
Phone: (919) 967-0078
Fax: (919) 967-4026
E-mail: orders@nichegdn.com
Web site: www.nichegdn.com

Nichols Garden Nursery
1190 N. Pacific Highway
Albany, OR 97321-4580
Phone: (541) 928-9280
Fax: (800) 231-5306
E-mail: customersupport@
    nicholsgardennursery.com
Web site:
    www.nicholsgardennursery.com

Park Seed
1 Parkton Avenue
Greenwood, SC 29647-0001
Phone: (800) 845-3369
Fax: (800) 275-9941
E-mail: info@parkseed.com
Web site: www.parkseed.com

Pinetree Garden Seeds
P.O. Box 300
New Gloucester, ME 04260
Phone: (207) 926-3400
Fax: (888) 527-3337
E-mail: pinetree@superseeds.com
Web site: www.superseeds.com

Plant Delights Nursery, Inc.
9241 Sauls Road
Raleigh, NC 27603
Phone: (919) 772-4794
Fax: (919) 662-0370
E-mail: office@plantdel.com
Web site: www.plantdel.com

Prairie Moon Nursery
R.R. #3, Box 163
Winona, MN 55987
Phone: (507) 452-1362
Fax: (507) 454-5238
Web site:
    www.prairiemoonnursery.com

Prairie Nursery
P.O. Box 306
Westfield, WI 53964
Phone: (800) 476-9453
Fax: (608) 296-2741
Web site: www.prairienursery.com

Roslyn Nursery
211 Burrs Lane
Dix Hills, NY 11746
Phone: (631) 643-9347
Fax: (631) 427-0894
E-mail: roslyn@roslynnursery.com
Web site: www.roslynnursery.com

Seeds Blüm
27 Idaho City Stage Road
Boise, ID 83716
Phone: (800) 742-1423
Fax: (208) 338-5658
E-mail:
    103374.167@compuserve.com
Web site: www.seedsblum.com

Seeds of Change
P.O. Box 15700
Sante Fe, NM 87506-5700
Phone: (888) 762-7333
Fax: (888) 329-4762
E-mail:
    gardener@seedsofchange.com
Web site:
    www.seedsofchange.com

Select Seeds Antique Flowers
180 Stickney Hill Road
Union, CT 06076
Phone: (860) 684-9310
Fax: (800) 653-3304
E-mail: info@selectseeds.com
Web site: www.selectseeds.com

Shepherd's Garden Seeds
30 Irene Street
Torrington, CT 06790-6658
Phone: (860) 482-3638
E-mail:
    custsrv@shepherdseeds.com
Web site: www.shepherdseeds.com

Stokes Seeds Inc.
P.O. Box 548
Buffalo, NY 14240-0548
Phone: (716) 695-6980
Fax: (716) 695-9649
E-mail: Stokes@stokeseeds.com
Web site: www.stokeseeds.com

Territorial Seed Co.
P.O. Box 157
Cottage Grove, OR 97424-0061
Phone: (541) 942-9547
Fax: (541) 942-9881
E-mail: tertrl@srv1.vsite.com
Web site:
    www.territorial-seed.com

Thompson and Morgan, Inc.
P.O. Box 1308
Jackson, NJ 08527-0308
Phone: (800) 274-7333
Fax: (888) 466-4769
E-mail:
    tminc@thompson-morgan.com
Web site:
    www.thompson-morgan.com

Van Ness Water Gardens
2460 North Euclid Avenue
Upland, CA 91784-1199
Phone: (800) 205-2425
Fax: (909) 949-7217
E-mail: vnwg@vnwg.com
Web site: www.vnwg.com

Wayside Gardens
1 Garden Lane
Hodges, SC 29695-0001
Phone: (800) 845-1124
Fax: (800) 457-9712
E-mail:
    curator@waysidegardens.com
Web site:
    www.waysidegardens.com

We-Du Nurseries
Route 5, Box 724
Marion, NC 28752
Phone: (828) 738-8300
Fax: (828) 738-8131
E-mail: wedu@wnclink.com
Web site: www.we-du.com

White Flower Farm
P.O. Box 50
Litchfield, CT 06759-0050
Phone: (800) 255-2852
Fax: (860) 496-1418
E-mail:
    custserv@whiteflowerfarm.com
Web site:
    www.whiteflowerfarm.com

Wildseed Farms
P.O. Box 3000
425 Wildflower Hills
Fredericksburg, TX 78624-3000
Phone: (800) 848-0078
Fax: (830) 990-8090
E-mail: wsf@fbg.net
Web site:
    www.wildseedfarms.com

Woodlanders, Inc.
1128 Colleton Avenue
Aiken, SC 29801
Phone/Fax: (803) 648-7522

FRUITS AND BERRIES

Adams County Nursery, Inc.
26 Nursery Road
P.O. Box 108
Aspers, PA 17304
Phone: (717) 677-8105
Fax: (717) 677-4124
E-mail: acn@cvn.net
Web site: www.acnursery.com

Bear Creek Nursery
P.O. Box 411
Northport, WA 99157
Phone: (509) 732-6219
Fax: (509) 732-4417
E-mail:
    info@bearcreeknursery.com
Web site:
    www.BearCreekNursery.com

**Country Carriage Nurseries and
    Seed, Inc.**
P.O. Box 548
Hartford, MI 49057
Phone: (616) 621-2491

Cummins Nursery
18 Glass Factory Bay Road
Geneva, NY 14456
Phone: (315) 789-7083
E-mail: jmc1@epix.net
Web site: www.dabney.com/
    cumminsnursery

Edible Landscaping
361 Spirit Ridge Lane
P.O. Box 77
Afton, VA 22920-0077
Phone: (804) 361-9134
Fax: (804) 361-1916
E-mail: el@cstone.net
Web site: www.eat-it.com

Hartmann's Plant Company
P.O. Box 100
Lacota, MI 49063-0100
Phone: (616) 253-4281
Fax: (616) 253-4457
E-mail: info@harmannsplant
    company.com
Web site: www.hartmannsplant
    company.com

Hidden Springs Nursery
170 Hidden Springs Lane
Cookeville, TN 38501
Phone: (931) 268-2592

Indiana Berry and Plant Co.
5218 West 500 South
Huntingburg, IN 47542
Phone: (800) 295-2226
Fax: (812) 683-2004
E-mail: berryinfo@inberry.com
Web site: www.inberry.com

Raintree Nursery
391 Butts Road
Morton, WA 98356
Phone: (360) 496-6400
Fax: (888) 770-8358
E-mail: customerservice@
    raintreenursery.com
Web site:
    www.raintreenursery.com

**Rocky Meadow Orchard &
    Nursery**
360 Rocky Meadow Road NW
New Salisbury, IN 47161
Phone: (812) 347-2213
Fax: (812) 347-2488
E-mail: rockymdw@netpointe.com

St. Lawrence Nurseries
325 S. H. 345
Potsdam, NY 13676
Phone: (315) 265-6739
E-mail: trees@sln.potsdam.ny.us
Web site: www.sln.potsdam.ny.us

Southmeadow Fruit Gardens
P.O. Box 211
10603 Cleveland Avenue
Baroda, MI 49101
Phone: (616) 422-2411
Fax: (616) 422-1464
E-mail: smfruit@aol.com

**Stark Bro's Nurseries and
    Orchards Co.**
P.O. Box 10, Dept. AB 1122 A9
Louisiana, MO 63353
Phone: (800) 478-2759
Fax: (573) 754-5290
E-mail: service@starkbros.com
Web site: www.starkbros.com

Van Well Nursery
P.O. Box 1339
Wenatchee, WA 98807
Phone: (509) 886-8189,
    (800) 572-1553
Fax: (509) 886-0294
E-mail: vanwell@vanwell.net
Web site: www.vanwell.net

Gardening Supplies and Tools

Alsto's Handy Helpers
Route 150 East
P.O. Box 1267
Galesburg, IL 61402-1267
Phone: (800) 447-0048
Fax: (800) 522-5786
E-mail:
    customerservice@alsto.com
Web site: www.alsto.com

The Beneficial Insect Co.
137 Forrest Street
Fort Mill, SC 29715
Phone: (803) 547-2301

Biocontrol Network
5116 Williamsburg Road
Brentwood, TN 37027
Phone: (615) 370-4301
Fax: (615) 370-0662
E-mail: info@biconet.com
Web site: www.biconet.com

BioSensory
Windham Mills Technology Center
322 Main Street, Building 1,
    2nd floor
Willimantic, CT 06226-3149
Phone: (860) 423-3009
Web site: www.biosensory.com

Bountiful Gardens
18001 Shafer Ranch Road
Willits, CA 95490-9626
Phone: (707) 459-6410
Fax: (707) 459-1925
E-mail: bountiful@sonic.net
Web site:
    www.bountifulgardens.org

W. Atlee Burpee and Co.
300 Park Avenue
Warminster, PA 18974
Phone: (800) 888-1447
Fax: (215) 674-4170
Web site: www.burpee.com

Charley's Greenhouse Supply
17979 State Route 536
Mount Vernon, WA 98273-3269
Phone: (800) 322-4707
Fax: (800) 233-3078
Web site:
    www.charleysgreenhouse.com

Delgard Aluminum Ornamental Fencing
Delair Group, Inc.
8600 River Road
Delair, NJ 08110
Phone: (800) 235-0185
Fax: (856) 663-1297
E-mail: info@delairgroup.com
Web site:
    www.delairgroup.com/delgard

Dripworks
190 Sanhedrin Circle
Willits, CA 95490
Phone: (800) 616-8321
Fax: (707) 459-9645
E-mail: dripwrks@pacific.net
Web site: www.dripworksusa.com
Drip irrigation products

Ehrlich Chemical Company
Magic Circle Deer Repellent
Donna Zerbee
500 Spring Ridge Drive
Reading, PA 19612
Phone: (610) 372-9700

agAccess/Fertile Ground Books
3912 Vale Avenue
Oakland, CA 94619-2222
Phone/Fax: (530) 298-2060
E-mail: books@agribooks.com
Web site: www.agribooks.com

Gardener's Supply Co.
128 Intervale Road
Burlington, VT 05401-2850
Phone: (888) 863-1700
Fax: (800) 551-1412
E-mail: info@gardeners.com
Web site: www.gardeners.com

Gardens Alive!
5100 Schenley Place
Lawrenceburg, IN 47025
Phone: (812) 537-8651
Fax: (812) 537-5108
E-mail:
    gardenhelp@gardens-alive.com
Web site: www.gardensalive.com

Harmony Farm Supply and Nursery
P.O. Box 460
Graton, CA 95444
Phone: (707) 823-9125
Fax: (707) 823-1734
E-mail: info@harmonyfarm.com
Web site: www.harmonyfarm.com

Johnny's Selected Seeds
RR 1, Box 2580
Foss Hill Road
Albion, ME 04910-9731
Phone: (207) 437-9294
Fax: (207) 437-2759
E-mail:
    johnnys@johnnyseeds.com
Web site: www.johnnyseeds.com

Kinsman Garden Co., Inc.
P.O. Box 357
River Road
Point Pleasant, PA 18950-0357
Phone: (800) 733-4146,
    (215) 297-0890
Fax: (215) 297-0450
E-mail: kinsmangarden@bux.com
Web site:
    www.kinsmangarden.com

Lehman's Catalog
One Lehman Circle
P.O. Box 41
Kidron, OH 44636
Phone: (888) 438-5346
Fax: (330) 857-5785
E-mail: info@lehmans.com
Web site: www.lehmans.com

A. M. Leonard, Inc.
241 Fox Drive
P.O. Box 816
Piqua, OH 45356-0816
Phone: (800) 543-8955
Fax: (800) 433-0633
E-mail: info@amleo.com
Web site: www.amleo.com

Max-Flex Fence Systems
U.S. Route 219
Lindside, WV 24951
Phone: (800) 356-5458
Fax: (304) 753-4827
E-mail: mail@maxflex.com
Web site: www.maxflex.com

The Natural Gardening Co.
P.O. Box 750776
Petaluma, CA 94975
Phone: (707) 766-9303
Fax: (707) 766-9747
E-mail:
    info@naturalgardening.com
Web site:
    www.naturalgardening.com

Natural Insect Control
RR#2
Stevensville, Ontario
L0S 1S0 Canada
Phone: (905) 382-2904
Fax: (905) 382-4418
E-mail: nic@niagara.com
Web site: www.natural-insect-
    control.com

N.I.M.B.Y.
DMX Industries
6540 Martin Luther King
St. Louis, MO 63133
Phone: (314) 385-0076
Fax: (314) 385-0062
E-mail: dmxinds@aol.com

Ohio Earth Food, Inc.
5488 Swamp Street, NE
Hartville, OH 44632
Phone: (330) 877-9356

Peaceful Valley Farm Supply
P.O. Box 2209
Grass Valley, CA 95945
Phone: (888) 784-1722,
    (530) 272-4769
Fax: (530) 272-4794
E-mail: contact@groworganic.com
Web site: www.groworganic.com

Pinetree Garden Seeds
Box 300
New Gloucester, ME 04260
Phone: (207) 926-3400
Fax: (888) 527-3337
E-mail:
    superseeds@worldnet.att.net
Web site: www.superseeds.com

Planet Natural
1612 Gold Avenue
Bozeman, MT 59715
Phone: (406) 587-5891
Fax: (406) 587-0223
E-mail: ecostore@mcn.net
Web site: www.planetnatural.com

Plow and Hearth
P.O. Box 5000
Madison, VA 22727-1500
Phone: (800) 627-1712
Fax: (800) 843-2509
Web site: www.plowhearth.com

**Pond and Landscape
    Solutions, Inc.**
2899 E. Big Beaver, #238
Troy, MI 48083
Fax: (248) 524-9059
E-mail: sales@pondsolutions.com
Web site: www.pondsolutions.com

**Saratoga Rail Fence and
    Supply Co.**
P.O. Box 13864
Albany, NY 12212-9600
Phone: (800) 869-8703
Fax: (518) 869-8755
PVC post and rail fencing

Seeds of Change
P.O. Box 15700
Sante Fe, NM 87506-5700
Phone: (888) 762-7333
Fax: (888) 329-4762
E-mail:
    gardener@seedsofchange.com
Web site:
    www.seedsofchange.com

H. B. Sherman Traps Inc.
3731 Peddie Drive
Tallahassee, FL 32303
Phone: (850) 575-8727
Fax: (850) 575-4864
E-mail: traps@shermantraps.com
Web site: www.shermantraps.com

Smith and Hawken
2 Arbor Lane, Box 6900
Florence, KY 41022-6900
Phone: (301) 771-4542
Fax: (301) 986-4829
E-mail: smithandhawkencustomer
    service@discovery.com
Web site:
    www.smithandhawken.com

The Tanglefoot Company
314 Straight Avenue SW
Grand Rapids, MI 49504-6485
Phone: (616) 459-4139
Fax: (616) 459-4140
E-mail: tnglfoot@aol.com
Web site: www.tanglefoot.com

Territorial Seed Co.
P.O. Box 157
Cottage Grove, OR 97424-0061
Phone: (541) 942-9547
Fax: (541) 942-9881
E-mail: tertrl@srv1.vsite.com
Web site:
    www.territorial-seed.com

Unilock New York, Inc.
51 International Boulevard
Brewster, NY 10509
Phone: (800) 864-5625
Fax: (914) 278-6788
E-mail: unilock@unilock.com
Web site: www.unilock.com
*Paving stones, retaining walls,
and curbing*

Whatever Works
Earth Science Building
74 20th Street
Brooklyn, NY 11232
Phone: (800) 499-6757
Fax: (718) 499-1005
Web site:
    www.whateverworks.com

Worm's Way
7850 N. Highway 37
Bloomington, IN 47404
Phone: (800) 274-9676
Fax: (800) 316-1264
E-mail: sales@wormsway.com
Web site: www.wormsway.com

HERBS

Fox Hollow Seed Co.
P.O. Box 148
McGrann, PA 16236
Phone: (412) 548-7333
Fax: (412) 543-5751

Gaia Garden Herbal Dispensary
2672 West Broadway
Vancouver, BC V6K 2G3
Canada
Phone: (604) 734-4372
Fax: (604) 734-4376
E-mail: herbs@gaiagarden.com
Web site: www.gaiagarden.com

Goodwin Creek Gardens
P.O. Box 83
Williams, OR 97544
Phone: (800) 846-7357
Fax: (541) 846-7357
E-mail: info@goodwincreek
    gardens.com
Web site: www.goodwincreek
    gardens.com

Horizon Herbs
P.O. Box 69
Williams, OR 97544
Phone: (541) 846-6704
Fax: (541) 846-6233
E-mail: herbseed@chatlink.com
Web site:
    www.chatlink.com/~herbseed

Johnny's Selected Seeds
RR1, Box 2580
Foss Hill Road
Albion, ME 04910-9731
Phone: (207) 437-4357
Fax: (207) 437-2759
E-mail: customerservice@johnny
    seeds.com
Web site: www.johnnyseeds.com

Long Creek Herbs
Route 4, Box 730
Oak Grove, AR 72660
Phone: (417) 779-5450
Fax: (417) 779-5450
E-mail: jim@longcreekherbs.com
Web site:
    www.longcreekherbs.com

Lunar Farms Herbals
3 Highland-Greenhills
Gilmer, TX 75644
Phone: (800) 687-1052
E-mail: spritsong1@aol.com
Web site:
    www.herbworld.com/lunarfarms

Nichols Garden Nursery
1190 N. Pacific Highway
Albany, OR 97321-4580
Phone: (541) 928-9280
Fax: (800) 231-5306
E-mail: customersupport@
    nicholsgardennursery.com
Web site:
    www.nicholsgardennursery.com

Richters Herb Catalogue
357 Highway 47
Goodwood, Ontario
L0C 1A0 Canada
Phone: (905) 640-6677
Fax: (905) 640-6641
E-mail: orderdesk@richters.com
Web site: www.richters.com

Sage Mountain Herbs
P.O. Box 420
E. Barre, VT 05649
Phone: (802) 479-9825
Fax: (802) 476-3722
E-mail: SageMtnHP@aol.com
Web site:
www.sagemountainherbs.com

The Sandy Mush Herb Nursery
Dept. OGRS
316 Surrett Cove Road
Leicester, NC 28748
Phone: (704) 683-2014

Shepherd's Garden Seeds
30 Irene Street
Torrington, CT 06790-6658
Phone: (860) 482-3638
E-mail:
custsrv@shepherdseeds.com
Web site:
www.shepherdseeds.com

Well-Sweep Herb Farm
205 Mt. Bethel Road
Port Murray, NJ 07865
Phone: (908) 852-5390
Fax: (908) 852-1649

SOIL TESTING

Cook's Consulting
R.D. 2, Box 13
Lowville, NY 13367
Phone: (315) 376-3002
*Organic recommendations, free
soil-testing kit*

Peaceful Valley Farm Supply
P.O. Box 2209
Grass Valley, CA 95945
Phone: (888) 784-1722,
(530) 272-4769
Fax: (530) 272-4794
E-mail: contact@groworganic.com
Web site: www.groworganic.com

Timberleaf Soil Testing Services
39648 Old Spring Road
Murrieta, CA 92563
Phone: (909) 677-7510
*Basic and trace mineral soil
tests; organic recommendations
provided*

Wallace Laboratories
365 Coral Circle
El Segundo, CA 90245
Phone: (310) 615-0116
Fax: (310) 640-6863
E-mail: contact@wallace-labs.com
Web site: www.wallace-labs.com

Woods End Research Laboratory
P.O. Box 297
Mt. Vernon, ME 04352
Phone: (800) 451-0337
Fax: (207) 293-2488
E-mail: weblink@woodsend.org
Web site: www.woodsend.org

TREES, SHRUBS, AND VINES

Carroll Gardens
444 E. Main Street
Westminster, MD 21157
Phone: (800) 638-6334
Fax: (410) 857-4112
Web site: www.carrollgardens.com

Forestfarm
990 Tetherow Road
Williams, OR 97544-9599
Phone: (541) 846-7269
Fax: (541) 846-6963
E-mail: orders@forestfarm.com
Web site: www.forestfarm.com

Greer Gardens
1280 Goodpasture Island Road
Eugene, OR 97401-1794
Phone: (541) 686-8266
Fax: (541) 686-0910
E-mail: orders@greegardens.com
Web site: www.greergardens.com

Gurney's Seed and Nursery Co.
110 Capital Street
Yankton, SD 57079
Phone: (605) 665-1671
Fax: (605) 665-9718
E-mail: info@gurneys.com
Web site: www.gurneys.com

Pickering Nurseries, Inc.
670 Kingston Road
Pickering, Ontario
L1V 1A6 Canada
Phone: (905) 839-2111
Fax: (905) 839-4807
Web site:
www.pickeringnurseries.com

ROSES

The Roseraie at Bayfields
P.O. Box R
Waldoboro, ME 04572-0919
Phone: (207) 832-6330
Fax: (800) 933-4508
E-mail: zapus@roseraie.com
Web site: www.roseraie.com

Roslyn Nursery
211 Burrs Lane
Dix Hills, NY 11746
Phone: (631) 643-9347
Fax: (631) 427-0894
E-mail: roslyn@roslynnursery.com
Web site: www.roslynnursery.com

Wayside Gardens
1 Garden Lane
Hodges, SC 29695-0001
Phone: (800) 845-1124
Fax: (800) 457-9712
E-mail:
curator@waysidegardens.com
Web site:
www.waysidegardens.com

White Flower Farm
P.O. Box 50
Litchfield, CT 06759-0050
Phone: (800) 255-2852
Fax: (860) 496-1418
E-mail:
    custserv@whiteflowerfarm.com
Web site:
    www.whiteflowerfarm.com

Woodlanders, Inc.
1128 Colleton Avenue
Aiken, SC 29801
Phone/Fax: (803) 648-7522

Vegetables

Abundant Life Seed Foundation
P.O. Box 772
Port Townsend, WA 98368
Phone: (360) 385-5660
Fax: (360) 385-7455
E-mail: abundant@olypen.com
Web site: csf.Colorado.edu/
    perma/abundant

Bountiful Gardens
18001 Shafer Ranch Road
Willits, CA 95490-9626
Phone: (707) 459-6410
Fax: (707) 459-1925
E-mail: bountiful@sonic.net
Web site:
    www.bountifulgardens.org

W. Atlee Burpee and Co.
300 Park Avenue
Warminster, PA 18974
Phone: (800) 888-1447
Fax: (215) 674-4170
Web site: www.burpee.com

Companion Plants
7247 N. Coolville Ridge Road
Athens, OH 45701
Phone: (740) 592-4643
Fax: (740) 593-3092
E-mail: complants@frognet.net
Web site:
    www.companionplants.com

The Cook's Garden
P.O. Box 535
Londonderry, VT 05148
Phone: (800) 457-9703
Fax: (800) 457-9705
E-mail:
    gardener@cooksgarden.com
Web site: www.cooksgarden.com

William Dam Seeds Ltd.
P.O. Box 8400
Dundas, Ontario
L9H 6M1 Canada
Phone: (905) 627-6641
Fax: (905) 627-1729
E-mail: willdam@sympatico.ca

Fedco Seeds
P.O. Box 520
Waterville, ME 04903
Phone: (207) 873-7333
Fax: (207) 872-8317
E-mail: fedco@mint.net

Ferry-Morse Seed Co.
P.O. Box 488
Fulton, KY 42041-0488
Phone: (800) 283-3400
Fax: (800) 283-2700
Web site: www.ferry-morse.com

Filaree Farm
182 Conconully Highway
Okanogan, WA 98840
Phone: (509) 422-6940
E-mail:
    filaree@northcascades.net
Web site: www.filareefarm.com

Fox Hollow Seed Co.
P.O. Box 148
McGrann, PA 16236
Phone: (412) 548-7333
Fax: (412) 543-5751

Garden City Seeds
778 Highway 93 N
Hamilton, MT 59840
Phone: (406) 961-4837
Fax: (406) 961-4877
E-mail: seeds@montana.com
Web site:
    www.gardencityseeds.com

Gurney's Seed and Nursery Co.
110 Capital Street
Yankton, SD 57079
Phone: (605) 665-1671
Fax: (605) 665-9718
E-mail: info@gurneys.com
Web site: www.gurneys.com

**Henry Field's Seed and
    Nursery Co.**
415 North Burnett
Shenandoah, IA 51602
Phone: (605) 665-4491
Fax: (605) 665-2601
E-mail: info@henryfields.com
Website: www.henryfields.com

Heritage Seed Co.
HC 78, Box 187
Star City, AR 71667
Phone: (870) 628-4820
E-mail: questions@daylilies.net

Ed Hume Seeds
P.O. Box 1450
Kent, WA 98035
Fax: (253) 859-0694
E-mail: HumeSeeds@aol.com
Web site: www.humeseeds.com

Irish Eyes with a Hint of Garlic
P.O. Box 307
Thorp, WA 98926
Phone: (509) 964-7000
Fax: (800) 964-9210
E-mail: potatoes@irish-eyes.com
Web site: www.irish-eyes.com

Johnny's Selected Seeds
RR1, Box 2580
Foss Hill Road
Albion, ME 04910-9731
Phone: (207) 437-4357
Fax: (207) 437-2759
E-mail: customerservice@
    johnnyseeds.com
Web site: www.johnnyseeds.com

Native Seeds/SEARCH
2509 N. Campbell Avenue # 325
Tucson, AZ 85719
Phone: (602) 327-9123

Nichols Garden Nursery
1190 N. Pacific Highway NE
Albany, OR 97321
Phone: (541) 928-9280
Fax: (541) 967-8406
E-mail: info@gardennursery.com
Web site: www.gardennursery.com

Park Seed
1 Parkton Avenue
Greenwood, SC 29647-0001
Phone: (800) 845-3369
Fax: (800) 275-9941
E-mail: orders@parkseed.com
Web site: www.parkseed.com

Pinetree Garden Seeds
P.O. Box 300
616A Lewiston Road
New Gloucester, ME 04260
Phone: (207) 926-3400
Fax: (888) 527-3337
E-mail:
    superseeds@worldnet.att.net
Web site: www.superseeds.com

Ronniger's Seed and Potato Co.
P.O. Box 1838
Orting, WA 98360
Phone: (860) 893-8782
Fax: (360) 893-3492

**Seed Savers Heirloom Seeds
    and Gifts**
3076 N. Winn Road
Decorah, IA 52101
Phone: (319) 382-5990
Fax: (319) 382-5872

Seeds Blüm
27 Idaho City Stage Road
Boise, ID 83716
Phone: (800) 742-1423
Fax: (208) 338-5658
E-mail:
    103374.167@compuserve.com
Web site: www.seedsblum.com

Seeds of Change
P.O. Box 15700
Sante Fe, NM 87506-5700
Phone: (888) 762-7333
Fax: (888) 329-4762
E-mail:
    gardener@seedsofchange.com
Web site: www.seedsofchange.com

**Seeds Trust, High Altitude
    Gardens**
P.O. Box 1048
Hailey, ID 83333-1048
Phone: (208) 788-4363
Fax: (208) 788-3452
E-mail: higarden@micron.net
Web site: www.seedsave.org

Shepherd's Garden Seeds
30 Irene Street
Torrington, CT 06790-6658
Phone: (860) 482-3638
Fax: (860) 482-0532
E-mail:
    custsrv@shepherdseeds.com
Web site: www.shepherdseeds.com

R. H. Shumway, Seedsman
P.O. Box 1
Graniteville, SC 29829-0001
Phone: (803) 663-9771
Fax: (888) 437-2733
Website: www.rhshumway.com

**Southern Exposure Seed
    Exchange**
P.O. Box 170
Earlysville, VA 22936
Phone: (804) 973-4703
Fax: (804) 973-8717
E-mail: gardens@
    southernexposure.com
Web site:
    www.southernexposure.com

Territorial Seed Co.
P.O. Box 157
Cottage Grove, OR 97424-0061
Phone: (541) 942-9547
Fax: (541) 942-9881
E-mail: tertrl@srv1.vsite.com
Web site:
    www.territorial-seed.com

**Tomato Growers Supply
    Company**
P.O. Box 2237
Fort Myers, FL 33902
Phone: (941) 768-1119
Fax: (888) 768-3476
Web site:
    www.tomatogrowers.com

Vermont Bean Seed Co.
Garden Lane
Fair Haven, VT 05743
Phone: (803) 663-0217
Fax: (888) 500-7333
E-mail: info@vermontbean.com
Web site: www.vermontbean.com

Willhite Seed Inc.
P.O. Box 23
Poolville, TX 76487
Phone: (817) 599-8656
Fax: (817) 599-5843
E-mail: info@willhiteseed.com
Web site: www.willhiteseed.com

Wood Prairie Farm
Jim and Megan Gerritsen
49 Kinney Road
Bridgewater, ME 04735
Phone: (207) 429-9765 or
    (800) 829-9765
Fax: (800) 300-6494
Web site: www.woodprairie.com

WILDFLOWERS

Abundant Life Seed Foundation
P.O. Box 772
Port Townsend, WA 98368
Phone: (360) 385-5660
Fax: (360) 385-7455
E-mail: abundant@olypen.com
Web site: csf.colorado.edu/
    perma/abundant

Clyde Robin Seed Co.
P.O. Box 2366
Castro Valley, CA 94546
Phone: (510) 785-0425
Fax: (510) 785-6463
Web site: www.clyderobin.com

Native Seeds/SEARCH
2509 N. Campbell Avenue # 325
Tucson, AZ 85719
Phone: (602) 327-9123

Plants of the Southwest
Agua Fria Road
Route 6, Box 11A
Santa Fe, NM 87501
Phone: (800) 788-7333
Fax: (505) 438-8800
E-mail: contact@plantsofthe
    southwest.com
Web site: www.plantsofthe
    southwest.com

Prairie Moon Nursery
Route 3, Box 163
Winona, MN 55987
Phone: (507) 452-1362
Fax: (507) 454-5238
Web site:
    www.prairiemoonnursery.com

Prairie Nursery
P.O. Box 306
Westfield, WI 53964
Phone: (800) 476-9453
Fax: (608) 296-2741
Web site: www.prairienursery.com

Wildseed Farms
P.O. Box 3000
425 Wildflower Hills
Fredericksburg, TX 78624-3000
Phone: (800) 848-0078
Fax: (830) 990-8090
Web site:
    www.wildseedfarms.com

Recommended Reading

COMPOSTING AND SOIL

Appelhof, Mary. *Worms Eat My Garbage.* Kalamazoo, MI: Flower Press, 1982.

Greshuny, Grace. *Start with the Soil.* Emmaus, PA: Rodale, 1993.

Hynes, Erin. *Rodale's Successful Organic Gardening: Improving the Soil.* Emmaus, PA: Rodale, 1994.

Martin, Deborah, and Grace Gershuny, eds. *The Rodale Book of Composting.* Emmaus, PA: Rodale, 1992.

Martin, Deborah, and Karen Costello Soltys, eds. *Rodale Organic Gardening Basics: Soil.* Emmaus, PA: Rodale, 2000.

GENERAL GARDENING

Benjamin, Joan, ed. *Great Garden Shortcuts.* Emmaus, PA: Rodale, 1996.

Bradley, Fern Marshall, and Barbara Ellis, eds. *Rodale's All-New Encyclopedia of Organic Gardening.* Emmaus, PA: Rodale, 1992.

Bucks, Christine, ed. *Rodale Organic Gardening Basics: Vegetables.* Emmaus, PA: Rodale, 2000.

Coleman, Eliot. *The New Organic Grower.* White River Junction, VT: Chelsea Green Publishing, 1995.

Costenbader, Carol W. *The Big Book of Preserving the Harvest.* Pownal, VT: Storey Communications, 1997.

Cunningham, Sally Jean. *Great Garden Companions.* Emmaus, PA: Rodale, 1998.

Lanza, Patricia. *Lasagna Gardening.* Emmaus, PA: Rodale, 1998.

Logsdon, Gene. *The Contrary Farmer's Invitation to Gardening.* White River Junction, VT: Chelsea Green Publishing, 1997.

Stone, Pat. *Easy Gardening 101.* Pownal, VT: Storey Communications, 1998.

Swain, Roger. *The Practical Gardener.* Boston: Little, Brown and Company, 1989. Reprint, New York: Galahad Books, 1998.

FRUITS AND BERRIES

McClure, Susan. *Rodale's Successful Organic Gardening: Fruits and Berries.* Emmaus, PA: Rodale, 1996.

Nick, Jean, and Fern Marshall Bradley. *Growing Fruits and Vegetables Organically.* Emmaus, PA: Rodale, 1994.

Reich, Lee. *Uncommon Fruits Worthy of Attention.* Reading, MA: Addison-Wesley Publishing, 1991.

HERBS

Duke, James A. *The Green Pharmacy*. Emmaus, PA: Rodale, 1997.

Gladstar, Rosemary. *Herbal Healing for Women*. New York: Simon & Schuster, 1993.

James, Tina. *The Salad Bar in Your Own Backyard*. Reisterstown, MD: Gardening from the Heart, 1996.

Kowalchik, Claire, and William H. Hylton. *Rodale's Illustrated Encyclopedia of Herbs*. Emmaus, PA: Rodale, 1987.

Long, Jim. *Herbs, Just for Fun: A Beginner's Guide to Starting an Herb Garden*. Oak Grove, AR: Long Creek Herbs, 1996.

———. *Classic Herb Blends*. Oak Grove, AR: Long Creek Herbs, 1996.

McClure, Susan. *The Herb Gardener: A Guide for All Seasons*. Pownal, VT: Storey Communication, 1995.

Oster, Maggie. *Herbal Vinegar*. Pownal, VT: Storey Communication, 1994.

Oster, Maggie, and Sal Gilbertie. *The Herbal Palate Cookbook*. Pownal, VT: Storey Communications, 1996.

Smith, Miranda. *Your Backyard Herb Garden*. Emmaus, PA: Rodale, 1997.

Sombke, Laurence. *Beautiful Easy Herbs*. Emmaus, PA: Rodale, 1997.

Tourles, Stephanie. *The Herbal Body Book*. Pownal, VT: Storey Communications, 1994.

LANDSCAPE AND FLOWER GARDENING

Bender, Steve, and Felder Rushing. *Passalong Plants*. Chapel Hill: The University of North Carolina Press, 1993.

Bradley, Fern Marshall, ed. *Gardening with Perennials*. Emmaus, PA: Rodale, 1996.

Byczynski, Lynn. *The Flower Farmer: An Organic Grower's Guide to Raising and Selling Cut Flowers*. White River Junction, VT: Chelsea Green Publishing, 1997.

Cox, Jeff. *Perennial All-Stars: The 150 Best Perennials for Great-Looking, Trouble-Free Gardens*. Emmaus, PA: Rodale, 1998.

D'Amato, Peter. *The Savage Garden: Cultivating Carnivorous Plants*. Berkeley, CA: Ten Speed Press, 1998.

DiSabato-Aust, Tracy. *The Well-Tended Perennial Garden: Planting and Pruning Techniques*. Portland, OR: Timber Press, 1998.

Ellis, Barbara. *Taylor's Guide to Growing North America's Favorite Plants*. Boston: Houghton Mifflin, 1998.

Harper, Pamela, and Frederick McGourty. *Perennials: How to Select, Grow and Enjoy*. Los Angeles: Price Stern Sloan, 1985.

McKeon, Judy. *The Encyclopedia of Roses*. Emmaus, PA: Rodale, 1995.

Phillips, Ellen, and C. Colston Burrell. *Rodale's Illustrated Encyclopedia of Perennials*. Emmaus, PA: Rodale, 1993.

Sombke, Laurence. *Beautiful Easy Flower Gardens*. Emmaus, PA: Rodale, 1995.

Taylor, Norman. *Taylor's Guide to Annuals*. Rev. ed. Boston: Houghton Mifflin, 1986.

Soltys, Karen Costello, ed. *Rodale Organic Gardening Basics: Roses*. Emmaus, PA: Rodale, 2000.

PEST MANAGEMENT

Ellis, Barbara W., and Fern Marshall Bradley. *The Organic Gardener's Handbook of Natural Insect and Disease Control*. Emmaus, PA: Rodale, 1992.

Gilkeson, Linda, et al. *Rodale's Pest and Disease Problem Solver*. Emmaus, PA: Rodale, 1996.

Hart, Rhonda. *Bugs, Slugs, and Other Thugs*. Pownal, VT: Storey Communications, 1991.

SEASON EXTENSION

Colebrook, Binda. *Winter Gardening in the Maritime Northwest*. Seattle, WA: Sasquatch Books, 1989.

Coleman, Eliot. *Four-Season Harvest: How to Harvest Fresh, Organic Vegetables from Your Home Garden All Year Long*. White River Junction, VT: Chelsea Green Publishing, 1992.

SEED STARTING

Bubel, Nancy. *The New Seed-Starter's Handbook*. Emmaus, PA: Rodale, 1988.

Ondra, Nancy, and Barbara Ellis. *Easy Plant Propagation*. (Taylor's Weekend Gardening Guides.) Boston: Houghton Mifflin, 1998.

Powell, Eileen. *From Seed to Bloom*. Pownal, VT: Storey Communications, 1995.

WEEDS

Hynes, Erin. *Rodale's Successful Organic Gardening: Controlling Weeds*. Emmaus, PA: Rodale, 1995.

Pleasant, Barbara. *The Gardener's Weed Book*. Pownal, VT: Storey Communications, 1996.

MAGAZINES AND NEWSLETTERS

Avant Gardener, The, P.O. Box 489, New York, NY 10028

Common Sense Pest Control Quarterly, Bio-Integral Resource Center (BIRC), P.O. Box 7414, Berkeley, CA 94707-0414

Country Living Gardener, 224 W. 57th Street, New York, NY 10019

Growing for Market, P.O. Box 3747, Lawrence, KS 66046

Homesteader's Connection, P.O. Box 5186, Cookeville, TN 38505

HortIdeas, 750 Black Lick Road, Gravel Switch, KY 40328

Organic Gardening, Rodale, 33 E. Minor Street, Emmaus, PA 18098

Index

USDA Plant Hardiness Zone Map

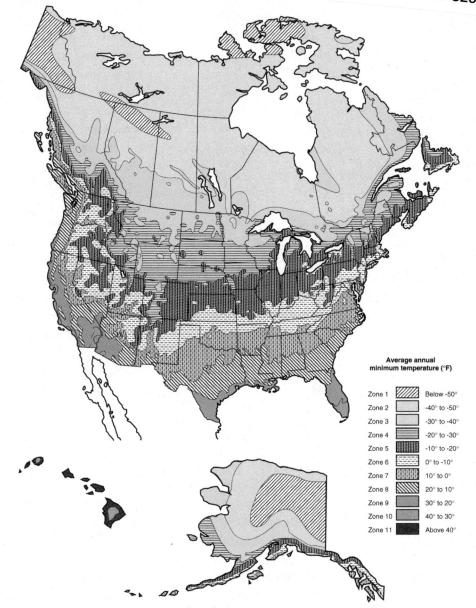

Average annual minimum temperature (°F)

Zone	Temperature
Zone 1	Below -50°
Zone 2	-40° to -50°
Zone 3	-30° to -40°
Zone 4	-20° to -30°
Zone 5	-10° to -20°
Zone 6	0° to -10°
Zone 7	10° to 0°
Zone 8	20° to 10°
Zone 9	30° to 20°
Zone 10	40° to 30°
Zone 11	Above 40°

This map was revised in 1990 and is recognized as the best indicator of minimum temperatures available. Look at the map to find your area, then match its color to the key. When you've found your color, the key will tell you what hardiness zone you live in. Remember that the map is a general guide; your particular conditions may vary.